DATE DUE

Objectives and Standards: An Approach to Planning and Control

OBJECTIVES AND STANDARDS

An Approach to Planning and Control

Ernest C. Miller

AMERICAN MANAGEMENT ASSOCIATION, INC.

This Research Study has been distributed without
charge to AMA members enrolled in the General
Management Division. Those members who are enrolled in other divisions, or who wish extra copies,
may order the Study at $7.00 per copy. Price to non-
members, $10.50.

Library of Congress catalog card number: 66-16863

MARY M. STANTON, *Editor*
SALLY B. HARRIMAN, *Assistant*

About This Report

In 1960 THE AMERICAN MANAGEMENT ASSOCIATION published the first major research report on *Setting Standards for Executive Performance*. This described the experiences and practices of a small group of innovative companies which had worked out and were using performance yardsticks for the work of their executives. Such standards may be described as "statements of conditions which exist when a job is being well done." They spell out a series of targets or expectations of a man and his supervisor in connection with a given job. They say *how well* rather than *what* is the job to be done.

The working out of such targets by constructive, earnest discussion between an executive and his chief has been found to offer the possibility of gaining a real feeling of commitment to achieve the targets. It is not surprising to find that in the years since 1960 many more companies have experimented with this standard-setting process. They have tried out a number of variations in approach. The intent of the present study has been to find out how well performance standards have worked and to report on the many significant refinements that have been found.

The same years have produced a surge of attention to business planning and control for the whole enterprise. A striking finding of the current research is that a number of companies have devised very successful processes for meshing key job targets (standards) with plans for the company as a whole. In so doing they have tied the standard-setting more closely to the energy and momentum of the day-to-day work and aims of the company.

The picture which emerges in the following report is one of real strides forward in the art of reconciling and aligning personal goals and company goals in ways that inspire executive action.

Many companies have contributed facts, ideas, and experiences to this study. Some are quoted or otherwise cited in the text of the report. The participants who gave so much help in our special research workshop on standards and objectives are identified in the list on the following page. Both to those mentioned by name and to those known only to the research staff, we all owe a debt; their sharing of experiences helps all managers to do better jobs.

ERNEST C. MILLER, author of this report and principal researcher in AMA's continuing study of the use of standards and objectives in the management process, has an extensive background in management and its study. He has been a member of the American Management Association's research staff since 1964. Earlier, he devoted nine years to consulting on problems of executive selection, training, and compensation, and organization planning and related general management concerns; three and a half years to helping a major international corporation establish its corporate personnel group; and four years to teaching at the University of Pennsylvania. He is author of papers on such subjects as long-range planning, policy development, the personnel audit, and executive performance appraisal. He is a Yale graduate with an M.A. from the University of Pennsylvania.

JOHN W. ENELL
Director of Research

The Workshop Participants

An AMA research workshop on the use of objectives and performance standards in management work provided much of the material for this research study. The workshop was arranged by Ernest C. Miller, AMA Research Project Leader—Standards, who also served as chairman of the discussion sessions. At the time of the workshop, the company titles of the participants were as listed below.

Clyde O. DeLong
Assistant to the President
The B.F. Goodrich Company

Betty A. Duval
Manager, Personnel Development
General Foods Corporation

Charles H. Granger
Partner
William E. Hill & Company, Inc.

Clarence Gray
Area Personnel Supervisor
General Electric Company
Evendale Plant

Robert Haugan
Vice President
Webb Publishing Company

Peter M. Herman
Manager, Methods and Standards
American Airlines

John Mastran
Manager, Organization Planning
    and Management Development
Radio Corporation of America

Dale D. McConkey
Vice President and Assistant to the President
United Fruit Company

T. B. Palmer
Vice President, Personnel
Yarway Corporation

John J. Simpkins
Manager, Management Services
Metropolitan Life Insurance Company

Oakley Turner
Manager of Transportation-Cleveland
The Standard Oil Company (Ohio)

Charles J. Wielgus
Director of Organization Development
The Reuben H. Donnelley Corporation

Contents

Company Forms

Table

Exhibits

1. The Management Process

As a business grows ever larger and more complex in today's competitive world, management's need to assign responsibility for results becomes even more urgent, for the work of the many individual managers of a company adds up to the total profitability of the enterprise. Managers must be motivated; their work must be coordinated and controlled; and the results must be evaluated in the light of the goals of the business. Don G. Mitchell, chairman of the board, General Time Corporation, has set forth the task in these words:

These people—these assets—will have little actual value unless they are motivated to do something, to function as a team that has clearly defined goals. Bearing in mind that management is the art of getting things done through people, you must remember that you can't get things done unless you let your people know what your goals are—what you want to accomplish, why you want to accomplish it, how they will benefit from it, and the role they will play in accomplishing it. This is another way of saying that the members of the management team must be able to identify themselves with the company's goals. No chief executive, no top management committee ever reached these goals unaided. Unless the entire management team is aboard, the company will never get where it wants to go.(1)*

_____
* Sources indicated in parentheses in the text are listed in full at the end of each chapter.

SUMMARY OF THE RESEARCH FINDINGS

The research described in this report was undertaken to discover what seem to be the most satisfactory means industry is now using to work out and agree on managerial goals. The experience and practice of major organizations in setting objectives and standards of performance for executives are reported in the following chapters. Briefly, here are some of the findings from interviews, a special research workshop, and questionnaire responses:

1. There have been significant changes in the techniques of planning and controlling the work of managers over the past five years, in most of the companies consulted.
2. The most common of these developments is toward directing the efforts of each executive to a smaller number of key targets in a given calendar period.
3. Truly challenging job objectives in limited number provide a sounder basis than an exhaustive cataloging of standards of performance can in organizing and controlling the work of a manager.
4. A smaller number of companies now use the approach of setting comprehensive sets of standards for all facets of each executive's job.

5. A substantial part of the value of a job objectives or standards program comes from the heightened motivation of the managers included in the program.

6. Of almost equal value is the improved communication of important, job-related information among managers at different levels and in different functions.

7. Managers can be selected, developed, and compensated more soundly when they are held accountable for performance against job objectives than by any other known approach.

8. Job objectives take logical and administrative precedence of budgets, organization plans, and management information systems.

9. Many companies find a program based on job objectives to be more easily linked with day-to-day work than is a program of standards of performance approached in the classical manner.

10. Practically all companies which have utilized the management-by-objectives approach report important gains in executive concentration on vital company targets.

THE ROLE OF JOB OBJECTIVES AND STANDARDS OF PERFORMANCE

"The management process," as the term is used in this report, refers to the day-to-day flow of decision making and control. Functional and job objectives and standards of performance are techniques for insuring the effective integration of an organization for direction and control according to overall objectives, and their planned use is the core of the management process.

Exhibit 1 shows the flow of ideas in organizing and planning for a business. Ideas flow from the environment—specifically,

from the needs of the customers the business sets out to serve—through the organization to the operative employees and then to the customers again. Represented in this exhibit are the decisions which must be made: the definition of the business; its philosophy, policies, and long-term objectives; and the objectives, plans, and standards for each of its major functions. Of highest interest are the flow and integration of long- and short-term objectives and plans and of corporate, unit, function, and job objectives, plans, and standards. The reciprocity of this flow at all levels and between the business and its customers is emphatic. The situation is dynamic and feedback is continuous. All decisions are subject to change. In most instances the more abstract decisions (the definition of the business, for example) will change less readily than will the concrete, operational decisions (such as staffing the northeastern sales region with three more salesmen during the year). Unit short-term objectives and plans influence and are influenced by the objectives, plans, and standards of each function and each of its jobs, and by customer needs. Unit objectives and plans must facilitate the work of each function as that work contributes to overall unit and corporate results, just as each function must set objectives, plans, and standards which will support the unit and the corporation.

Exhibit 2 depicts the translation of unit objectives and standards to a function and, through the manager of the function, to each of its jobs. The unit's objectives *A, B, C,* and *D* require a contribution from research and development. Each of the objectives relates to one of the job responsibilities of the manager of research and development; that is to say, he has the responsibility to act to help accomplish the desired result. This may be either a unilateral or a shared responsibility; if it is shared with other functions, the manager is jointly accountable

Exhibit 1. *Planning for a Business*

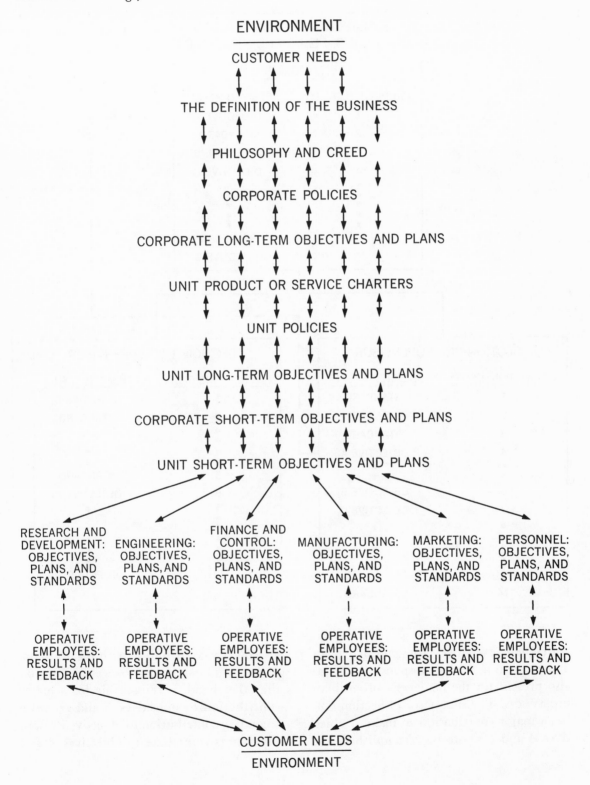

ENVIRONMENT

CUSTOMER NEEDS

THE DEFINITION OF THE BUSINESS

PHILOSOPHY AND CREED

CORPORATE POLICIES

CORPORATE LONG-TERM OBJECTIVES AND PLANS

UNIT PRODUCT OR SERVICE CHARTERS

UNIT POLICIES

UNIT LONG-TERM OBJECTIVES AND PLANS

CORPORATE SHORT-TERM OBJECTIVES AND PLANS

UNIT SHORT-TERM OBJECTIVES AND PLANS

| RESEARCH AND DEVELOPMENT: OBJECTIVES, PLANS, AND STANDARDS | ENGINEERING: OBJECTIVES, PLANS, AND STANDARDS | FINANCE AND CONTROL: OBJECTIVES, PLANS, AND STANDARDS | MANUFACTURING: OBJECTIVES, PLANS, AND STANDARDS | MARKETING: OBJECTIVES, PLANS, AND STANDARDS | PERSONNEL: OBJECTIVES, PLANS, AND STANDARDS |

| OPERATIVE EMPLOYEES: RESULTS AND FEEDBACK | OPERATIVE EMPLOYEES: RESULTS AND FEEDBACK | OPERATIVE EMPLOYEES: RESULTS AND FEEDBACK | OPERATIVE EMPLOYEES: RESULTS AND FEEDBACK | OPERATIVE EMPLOYEES: RESULTS AND FEEDBACK | OPERATIVE EMPLOYEES: RESULTS AND FEEDBACK |

CUSTOMER NEEDS

ENVIRONMENT

EXHIBIT 2. *Planning for a Function*

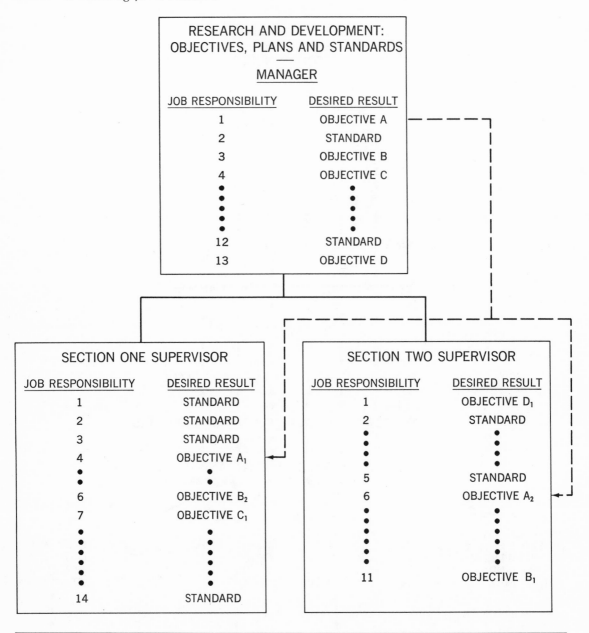

with their executives for producing the desired result. Similar responsibilities are also present for the manager's subordinate supervisors. The supervisor of Section One has a major contribution to make if objectives *A* and *C* are to be accomplished, and a secondary contribution with regard to objective *B*. The supervisor of Section Two, on the other hand, is responsible for a major contribution to objectives *B* and *D* and a secondary contribution to objective *A*. Both supervisors contribute to objectives *A* and

Exhibit 3. *Planning for a Job*

RESEARCH AND DEVELOPMENT: SECTION ONE SUPERVISOR
WORK PLAN

JOB RESPONSIBILITY	DESIRED RESULT	PRESENT CONDITION	PLAN	PRIORITY
1	STANDARD	20% BETTER THAN STANDARD	REDUCE BUDGET 10%	3
2	STANDARD	STANDARD	NO CHANGE	5
3	STANDARD	3% BETTER THAN STANDARD	NO CHANGE	5
4	OBJECTIVE A_1	1% BETTER THAN OBJECTIVE	NO CHANGE	5
⋮				
6	OBJECTIVE B_2	15% BELOW OBJECTIVE	INCREASE BUDGET & STAFF 15%	2
7	OBJECTIVE C_1	NO CAPABILITY	PROVIDE STAFF	4
⋮				
14	STANDARD	10% BELOW STANDARD	INCREASE BUDGET & STAFF 15%	1

B; objectives *C* and *D,* however, have been delegated to one or the other.

If a job is not being performed "at standard" for each of its responsibilities, the job responsibilities for which results are below —or above—standard level will be incorporated in unit or functional objectives and plans for that job. For all jobs there is a continuing general objective of discharging all responsibilities at least at standard level; the job responsibilities at variance from standard become added job objectives. And, in turn, these become objectives of the unit and function.

How a job incumbent would review his past performance and plan his work for the next period (in most cases this will be done in conjunction with his supervisor) is shown in Exhibit 3, which is the work plan of the Section One supervisor of Exhibit 2. Four items merit particular note:

1. Job responsibility 14, with results 10 percent below standard, is a 1 priority activity and merits a 15 percent increase in budget and staff.

2. Job responsibility 6 contributes to unit objective B_2, and—since present results are 15 percent below the level set in the objective—is a 2 priority activity calling for a 15 percent increase in budget and staff.

3. Job responsibility 1 is being per-

Basis of the Research

The information which was the basis for this report was collected from four sources:

- Interviews with 35 executives in 30 leading U.S. organizations known to use or to have used objectives and/or standards of performance.
- A research workshop attended by 12 representatives of U.S. companies which have had success with their approaches to the use of these techniques.
- The 71 responses to a questionnaire mailed to 128 U.S. and Canadian companies which had sent representatives to AMA seminars on standards of performance, management by results, or management by objectives, from 1962 to early 1965.
- A review of business literature.

All major industries are represented in the companies from which useful information was obtained concerning their applications of these management techniques.

The respondents' companies range in size from about $2 million a year in annual sales to more than $1 billion. Although most of the companies interviewed were in the New York City area, the report is based on the experiences of companies in every part of the United States and eastern Canada.

No effort was made to sample present industry practice in using or not using objectives and standards of performance. Our interest was in learning the experiences of users.

---

formed 20 percent better than standard, which permits a budget reduction of 10 percent.

4. Job responsibility 4 covers objective A_1, but since present performance is 1 percent better than the objectives, no special action is required.

With the feedback from the work plans to successively higher organization levels and the consequent revision in objectives and plans necessary at each level to adjust to what is actually taking place, the management process is completed.

REPORTS FROM USERS OF OBJECTIVES
AND PERFORMANCE STANDARDS

What results have been achieved through the use of objectives and performance stand-ards in managing? The participants in the research differ, naturally, in the basis for their judgment on the subject and in their criteria for success with these techniques. Their citations are estimates and subjective evaluations; yet there is an impressive consistency in their reports that investment in an objectives or standards program is worthwhile.

Approval based on experience was expressed by E. H. Fallon, executive vice president, Agway, Inc. He listed the following benefits to his company:

1. Considerable improvement in coordinated effort toward established company goals.
2. Considerable improvement in individual performance, as the result of objectives combined with appraisals.

3. Considerable improvement in understanding and team effort.

A similar opinion was voiced by L. F. Zerfoss, director of management services, American Enka Corporation, who described the results expected by his company's management: "Management expects more from its people and is getting more; more pressure, more results-orientation, more tautness, more tightening up. We're out to reduce inhibitions to effort and to get higher motivation—we believe this is in the right direction."

In the opinion of Joseph T. Gresh, assistant director of management personnel, American Brake Shoe Company, the major contribution of the approach his company uses is that it helps the company's managers to be less subjective and more objective. The firm considers the objective approach essential to a sound effort. Mr. Gresh spoke further on this theory as follows:

The divisions that have the program now are enthusiastic about it. They think it adds greatly to what they are doing and they like the fact that it is work-related. Also, they value the help it has given them to communicate and reach agreement on the job and the important elements of it. They frequently say that, before, they really didn't understand what was expected of them. As an example: one man (who had been vice president of sales for ten years), on receiving the approved statement of responsibilities and standards from his boss—statements to which he himself had contributed—said, "This is the first time in the ten years I've been on this job that I really understand what my job is. I never before really knew what I was supposed to do, or how I would be measured.

C. J. Gauthier, executive vice president, Northern Illinois Gas Company, has a different but equally interesting viewpoint:

The benefits accruing to our public are self-evident:

1. Our employees are the highest paid in the industry.

2. The market appraisal of our securities is the most favorable in the industry.
3. Our customers have experienced sizable decreases in cost of product and service in a period when most industries, including our own, have had to raise costs.

From a similar standpoint, a representative of RCA described the excellent results from their program, in which specific goals are set against each job responsibility. It was reported that one "results-oriented" general manager in RCA gave his industrial engineers and cost accountants the assignment of evaluating the goals that had been set. They came up with the estimate that, if all the goals were achieved, the division would add $500,000 to profit. And what were the actual results? According to this company spokesman, 80 percent of the goals were achieved and $400,000 was added to profit.

Still other benefits to their companies as a result of the use of objectives and standards of performance were briefly listed by respondents:

- Greater unity of purpose throughout the company.
- Increased manager motivation.
- Improved self-direction and self-control in managers.
- Creation of a more demanding, more highly charged company tone.
- Improved communication.
- Closer cooperation and coordination.
- A sounder basis for executive appraisal and development.
- Clearer standards for control decisions.
- A sounder basis for compensation decisions.

NOTE TO CHAPTER 1

1. Mitchell, Don G., "The Challenges Facing Management," The Charles C. Moskowitz Lectures, School of Commerce, Accounts and Finance, New York University, New York University Press, 1963, p. 30.

2. Systems and Control

In THE PAST 20 YEARS OUR CONceptual skills have developed to a level at which we can understand and cope successfully with a major business activity considered as an adaptive and striving organism. Increased ability to measure related aspects of business, both within a company and in its environment, have made possible the scientific study of phenomena that previously could be only described.

While it is beyond the scope of this study to delve deeply into systems theory, a brief introduction to its implications for management is appropriate here.

Current thinking stresses the value of visualizing business as a "system." The development of the concept of cybernetics—the science of communication and control—provided the essential model of a system. In the simplest models these cybernetic systems attempted to minimize performance variations around a control value—in management terms, a "standard."

Stafford Beer, an English writer on cybernetics as applied to industrial management, has said:

Anything that consists of parts connected together will be called a system. For instance, a game of snooker is a system, whereas a single snooker ball is not. A car, a pair of scissors, an economy, a language, an ear, and a quadratic equation: all these things are systems. They can be pointed out as aggregates of bits and pieces; but they begin to be understood only when the connections between the bits and pieces, the dynamic interactions of the whole organism, are made the object of study.(1)

In other words, it is the factor of connectiveness—"the dynamic interactions of the whole organism"—that makes a system. Since connectiveness exists among all units of a company and between the company and its environment, taken all together these elements constitute a system. But any unit of this overall system is also a system—or, as it is commonly called, a "subsystem"—which is related to all the other units and to the system itself. What will be included in the system has, for each element, its own definition which will take into consideration functional, geographic, or technological integrations.

The linkages between the "bits and pieces" of a system are "communication"; "information" is carried along these linkages; action derived from this information constitutes a "decision." And when the information in a system consists of measurements of system performance against objectives and standards, this information provides the basis for feedback and control.

APPLICATIONS TO MANAGEMENT

Emphasis on the whole organism is the essence of industrial dynamics. A recent article in *Business Week* described the industrial dynamics program at MIT (where Jay W. Forrester, a professor of industrial management, did much to launch the movement):

The new program is heavily committed to a systems approach—forcing attention on an organization as a whole, not as a series of unrelated parts. This philosophy runs through the entire program, even down to simulating business systems by computer.(2)

The manager's job has also been defined in terms of systems. To quote from an article by Seymour Tilles in *Harvard Business Review:*

The manager's work divides into four basic tasks:
1. Defining the company as a system.
2. Establishing system objectives, which can be further broken down to:
   • Identifying wider systems.
   • Setting performance criteria.
3. Creating formal subsystems.
4. Systemic integration.(3)

In managing a business, as in all purposeful activity, there is a general control cycle whose elements can be precisely stated. J. M. Juran has described this cycle in these words:

. . . There is an unvarying sequence of steps which is necessary to regulate anything, this sequence being as follows:
1. Selection of control points.
2. Definition of units of measure.
3. A systematic means for measuring and summarizing actual performance.
4. Selection of standards of performance.
5. Interpretation of the difference between actual performance and standard.
6. Decision on what action to take.
7. Action to comply with the decision.(4)

Westinghouse Electric Corporation's brochure (5), uses a simplified schematic representation of the systems approach (Exhibit 4). This diagram of the management cycle shows a review stage in which objectives and performance standards are used, and a feedback stage in which reports based on the comparison of results achieved with results expected are made.

OBJECTIVES DEFINED

Though differing in the expression of their definitions, most of the organizations consulted in the research for this report are essentially in agreement on the meaning of the most frequently used terms—"management by objectives," "job objectives," "key results," "performance standards." Metropolitan Life Insurance Company, for example, sets forth broadly but concisely what it means by "management by objectives," and what it expects to gain from it:

"Management by objectives" describes the management process whereby all work is organized in terms of achieving specified conditions (results) by set times. Implicit in the process is the requirement that the specified conditions contribute to achieving the broader objectives of the organization.(6)

Charles H. Granger, partner, William E. Hill & Company, Inc., is equally succinct in speaking of the purpose and use of objectives: "An objective is an aim or end of action; it is also used as an aim or guide to intermediate decisions and actions."(7)

The Air Force Logistics Command states its definition of job objectives with military explicitness:

A job objective is a statement of personal commitment to a specific accomplishment or result that is:
• Oriented to mission.
• Measurable.

EXHIBIT 4. *The Management Cycle in a Systems View of Managing*

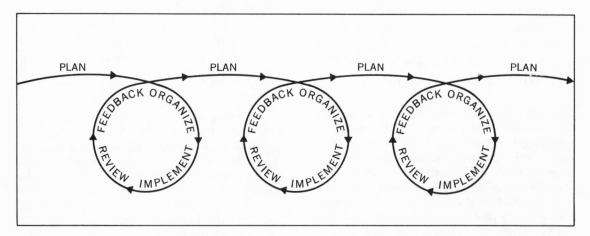

• Needed.
• Valuable (that is, equal to or greater in value than the man-hours, monies, materials, and facilities needed to create the product).
• Time-phased for accomplishment.(8)

American-Standard defines "key results" in terms of what is *expected* in key result targets and the individual's contribution to their attainment:

. . . the key results . . . represent the major accomplishments which are required from [the individual] if the component for which he is responsible is to make its budgeted profit contribution. Key result targets should embrace the total responsibility of the individual. . . . To be authorized, result targets must:
1. Be specific as to exactly what is to be accomplished and by when.
2. State expected results in positive, measurable terms.
3. List the *results* to be accomplished, not just the activities leading to them; indicate *what*, not *how*.
4. Establish definite, forward-looking goals in each major area of the manager's responsibility. These must cover his total responsibility.
5. Be sufficiently difficult of attainment to require a high level of managerial effort, but not so difficult as to be impossible of attainment.

6. Be directly tied into the annual profit plan, and call for full accomplishment thereof.(9)

Like American-Standard and the Air Force, a large chemical company which took part in the research stresses the requirement that a statement of an objective must specify a time limit within which the objective is to be met:

An objective is a statement of the *desired or needed result* to be achieved by a *specified time*. It should be worthy of attainment, yet capable of achievement by superior performance.

Department objectives should be set knowing that both staff units and profit centers will receive credit for results where each has contributed toward the achievement.

Objectives should be set in those areas where results are essential to the continued prosperity of the business enterprise.

It is probable that most companies which practice management by objectives set forth their policy in a formal statement, whether the statement is brief and general or long and detailed. There are executives, however, who feel that their managers function more freely and fruitfully in the absence of formal policy; in other words, that in an effective organizational climate management by objectives does not need to be talked about, for it is being carried on anyway. Such a one is John Paul Jones (general manager, organization development, Union Carbide Corporation), who states this opinion:

The thing we really need to do is to develop relationships of mutual trust and respect. We need to get people to the point where they are secure and free enough to say what they really think to relate freely with each other with no fear of retribution. When you get a group that has achieved this sitting around a table, dealing with business problems, what do you find them doing? They talk about where they are and where they want to go. They talk about how long it ought to take them and what must specifically be done to get there. They talk about how they will know what progress they are making. They make arrangements for feedback. In other words, they may not use the words *but they are managing and using objectives.* It is a natural process; people faced with a complex job to do will use it. You don't have to give it a name. That just formalizes it. Then people get committed for or against the words "management by objectives" and may lose sight of what they are really trying to achieve.

DEFINITIONS OF STANDARDS

Companies which have set up formal standards of performance for their managers often include them in a general policy and procedures manual. One such firm is Connecticut General Life Insurance Company, which introduces the standards section of its manual with the following definition:

A performance standard (sometimes called a job standard) is a statement of conditions that will exist when a job is satisfactorily done. It completes the statement: "This job will have been satisfactorily performed when the following results are obtained. . . ."

A performance standard emphasizes results; it makes the person accountable for the results of

what he does. It is a statement of what constitutes adequate work.(10)

In defining standards of performance Virgil K. Rowland, in his book, *Standards of Performance,* states the case for *written* standards:

. . . The boss . . . has a picture in his mind of the conditions that will exist when the company—which in general means all of the managers in it—is doing a good job, and this picture is in reality a composite of the conditions that exist when each department, and each manager within each department, is doing well. One of the best ways to transfer that picture into the minds of his subordinates is to translate it into writing.

A standard of performance will be defined here, therefore, as "a written statement of conditions that will exist when a job is being well done."(11)

To Rowland's definition J. W. Enell and G. H. Haas add a statement on the content of standards:

. . . standards of performance say *how well,* rather than *what.* They spell out the targets or expectations of a man and his supervisor in connection with a given job. Through analysis of each major job segment, a series of standards or specific goals for performance is developed. These can be used later to judge whether or not the total job is being performed satisfactorily. Meanwhile they represent an agreement on the goals of the job holder.(12)

And J. M. Juran, in *Managerial Breakthrough,* comments on the various terms used to mean "standards" in different functions:

Standards are all over, though they masquerade under a variety of aliases.

In the market, the standard for "How much should I sell?" is called a "quota."

In the laboratory, the standard for "How much should it measure?" is called a "specification."

In the office, the standard for "How much should I spend?" is called a "budget."

On the shop floor, the standard for "When should I deliver?" is called a "schedule."

And so on—target, piece rate, goal, aim, intent. The dialect varies, but the meaning is the same.

Sometimes a single term is adopted to represent any standard. In Koppers Company, the term "program" was used to represent any target, whether for earnings, sales, inventories, etc.(13)

From the policies and practices of these and the other sources of the research, the following definitions have been drawn by the author for the purposes of this report.

"Job objective" refers to a desired improvement in results. It is realistic, feasible, and specific. It sets a target for accomplishment in a specified time period. It is results-oriented and closely related to the economic success of the business and, therefore, to its budgets and profit plans.

"Standard of performance" describes the conditions that will be present when a job is well done. Such a standard covers the major responsibilities of a job and is realistic, feasible, and specific. It is control-oriented. Although it is related to the economic success of the business and, therefore, to its budgets and profit plans, a close relationship will not always be present.

NOTES TO CHAPTER 2

1. Beer, Stafford, *Cybernetics and Management,* John Wiley & Sons, Inc., New York, 1959, p. 9.
2. "At MIT, Students Are the Boss," *Business Week,* January 23, 1965, p. 82.
3. Tilles, Seymour, "The Manager's Job: A Systems Approach," *Harvard Business Review,* January 1963, p. 74.
4. Juran, J. M., "Universals in Management Planning and Controlling," THE MANAGEMENT REVIEW, November 1954, p. 755.
5. *Career Development in Management,* Training Department, Management and Professional Services, Westinghouse Electric Corporation, Pittsburgh, Pa.
6. "Management by Objectives," Management Services Department, Metropolitan Life Insurance Company, New York, 1965.
7. Granger, Charles, "The Hierarchy of Objectives," *Harvard Business Review,* May-June 1964, p. 63.
8. *Results-Oriented Management: "Management by (Job) Objectives,"* Air Force Logistics Command, AFLC Pamphlet 25-2, November 7, 1962.
9. "Appraising the Performance of Exempt Salaried Employees," American Radiator & Standard Sanitary Corporation, New York, September 28, 1960, pp. 2-3.
10. "Performance Standards," *Standard Practices and Procedures Manual,* Connecticut General Life Insurance Company, Hartford, Conn., February 23, 1961, p. 310.
11. Rowland, Virgil K., *Managerial Performance Standards,* American Management Association, 1960, pp. 35-36.
12. Enell, J. W., and George H. Haas, *Setting Standards for Executive Performance,* Research Study No. 42, American Management Association, 1960, p. 16.
13. Juran, J. M., *Managerial Breakthrough,* McGraw-Hill Book Co., New York, 1964, p. 234.

3. Setting up the Program: The Framework

To DEFINE THE BUSINESS IS the very first act of the objective-setting effort; in a sense, the formal definition tells *the* objective of the whole enterprise. Companies which are sophisticated in their approach to planning, therefore, start with such a statement when they prepare to set up a program of management by objectives or standards of performance.

Developing the definition, however it is expressed, is the task of the executive board and top management, for it is only at top level that the knowledge of broad economic needs and of the special competitive resources of the company are to be found.

MANAGEMENT CREEDS AND POLICIES; CHARTERS

The nature of the business is frequently expressed in terms of the company's "mission." Louis T. Rader, vice president, General Electric Company, calls this understanding of purpose "vision for the business," which, he says:

. . . is the hard work involved in establishing an identity for the business which distinguishes it from competition. This identity, this *knowledge of self,* can then be used dynamically and aggressively as a focus to pinpoint markets, competitors, and resources in terms of the pivotal entrepreneurial decisions currently needed.

Any model of a business constructed without consideration of this input is likely to be a creation that responds only defensively to the environment.(1)

A statement of mission may be formally phrased, or on the other hand it may be an expression of overall intent, the cumulative result of informal utterances of the president. Even where it is not stated formally, most companies do try to achieve an agreed understanding among their managers as to what the company is and what it seeks to accomplish. Xerox Corporation's mission, for example, has been thus informally described by its president, Joseph C. Wilson. This statement also includes a reference to the company's public responsibility.

When people ask me what Xerox really wants to do, I say we want to render values, usually new ones that men have not enjoyed before.

We want to be part of an industry that gives men something worth getting. We want to add new dimensions to the ways they communicate, to make increasing knowledge more broadly useful. We want to profit from these efforts. And we want those associated with us to be proud of what they are doing.

23

Our means are sometimes unusual, and we deeply believe that to stay in front, our goals must stretch beyond the sight horizon of a single year's balance sheet or even a single decade's.

To say we are in the communications business suggests, at least to us, an obligation to a world in which people *can* communicate. It suggests the need for freedom and peace, and it demands the end of ignorance. If man is to progress, knowledge must spread freely throughout the world.

This is the reason, for example, Xerox gives 1 percent of its net income before taxes to support higher education. It is the reason we sponsor television programs that raise deep, serious issues.

Acts like these cause controversy.

But controversy is the inevitable price of meeting issues and of innovation. I can't help but remember the wisdom of Robert Frost:

> Two roads diverged in a wood, and I—
> I took the one less traveled by,
> And that has made all the difference.

The road chosen by Xerox is one "less traveled by," but it seems to be leading steeply upward.(2)

More specifically, a statement of mission may be used to give direction to management's efforts within the company. The Boeing Company, for example, has assigned this mission to one of its divisions: "The mission of electronics operations is to develop into an expanding and profitable entity for the full support of company programs and to compete in selected areas of prime electronics business."(3)

The definition of the business sets the direction. As a further step in informing managers what the company is like before they are told what their part in the business is, many companies draw up creeds for general guidance.

The broad ethical tone of a company creed is the primary factor that distinguishes it from a statement of mission or definition of the business. The second difference is that, by reason of these ethical and moral considerations which influence the choice of means, creeds represent constraints rather more than impetus. It is this aspect of their use that Stewart Thompson, in *Management Creeds and Philosophies,* has emphasized in his definition: "A 'company creed' . . . may be thought of as the most basic sort of guiding statement of company objectives which also *lays down the ethical practices to be adhered to in achieving these objectives.*"(4) In his book, which is a survey of top management guides in our changing economy, Thompson lists the purposes stated by respondents for developing creeds used by their companies:

1. To define the purpose of the company. (To state exactly why the firm is in business.)
2. To clarify the philosophy-character of the company. (To state the moral and ethical principles guiding its actions.)
3. To create a particular "climate" within the business. (To communicate the basic purposes and ethics of the company to all those in company ranks so that they may communicate them to customers and others outside the firm through their actions.)
4. To set down a guide for managers so that the decisions they make will reflect the best interests of the business with fairness and justice to those concerned. (To provide an overall guide to those in decision-making positions so that they can act independently but within the framework of the firm's basic goals and principles.)(5)

Two brief creeds quoted by Thompson are reproduced here. The first of the two meets all four purposes listed above; the second poses ethical questions to be asked of basic policy.

Atlas Steels Limited

—To achieve as high a return upon investment as is possible, compatible with firm Christian principles, scrupulous honesty, and complete fairness to *all* people whom we contact—especially shareholders, employees, customers, and suppliers.(6)

Sorensen & Company Incorporated Creed

First...........................Is it the truth?

Second......................Is it fair to all concerned?

Third.......................Will it build goodwill?

Fourth.....................Will it be beneficial to all concerned?(7)

Policies also are constraints on the company in that they guide the choice of means to be used in reaching objectives. However, in distinction from creeds, policies express no special ethical or moral tone. General Electric Company defines a policy as "a definition of common purposes for organization components, or the company as a whole, in matters where, in the interest of achieving both component and overall company objectives, it is desirable that those responsible for implementation exercise discretion and good judgment in appraising and deciding among alternate courses of action."(8)

In many large firms the statement of mission is included in a policy document called a "charter," which describes the business of a division or a profit center in more detail. The charter may define the customers the company serves; the scope of products; the specific activity; and relationships with company departments. One large chemical company defines a charter in these words.

A charter is a written delineation of the nature and scope of the business and intracompany relationships of a profit center. It is a description of the boundaries of the profit center's responsibilities and opportunities.

Because it is a point of agreement between corporate, divisional, and profit center management, it is subject to modification only by corporate management. It is incumbent, however, upon profit center and division management to request modification as changing conditions warrant.

This charter indicates a concept similar to that of General Electric, whose organization book states: "One basic purpose of . . . a business charter . . . is to help avoid confusion, interferences, overlaps, or omissions among departments, with regard to products, functions, markets, and resources."(9) Charters are assigned to groups, divisions, and departments in the General Electric complex to insure the proper integration of activities in the company's effort to accomplish its stated mission: "To carry on a diversified, growing, and profitable worldwide manufacturing business in electrical apparatus, appliances, and supplies, and in related materials, products, systems, and services for industry, commerce, agriculture, government, the community, and the home."(10)

KEY RESULTS AREAS

Most companies, as soon as they have defined the broad lines of the framework in which they will operate, identify the activities they judge to be critical to the long-term success of the business.

There has never been any lack of interest in identifying and measuring the key results areas of a business. Economists, naturally, are concerned; the issue touches the heart of their discipline. Owners have also had a natural interest, although this interest has not often been revealed in vigorous public discussion. With ownership diffused among many stockholders, with stock trading active, with professional security analysts delving deeper into a company's business performance, and with government agencies looking more closely at a company's contribution to the economy, it is easy to understand why professional managers have been seeking "hard" measures by which the company's performance and their own can be appraised.

Although the pattern for financing business expansion has been changing—specifically, more funds are now generated out of depreciation and retained earnings, and from borrowing rather than equity financing—managers retain a healthy respect for the standards the investment community uses in judging the quality of securities. To the investment community, key results mean earnings per share, growth of earnings per share, stability of earnings, and dividend payout. The prime objective, for most companies, is to be above their industry's averages on these measures. Charles Granger, a partner in William E. Hill & Company, management consultants, led a discussion at an AMA research workshop on management by objectives.* Mr. Granger began by inviting the participants to consider the objectives of a business enterprise:

What should the objectives of an enterprise be? Peter Drucker says, basically, that customer service should be the ultimate objective of the enterprise. Someone else believes it is profit. And at annual meetings a few stockholders may say the objectives are high dividends and low compensation. There are differences in point of view.

Suppose we are all on the board of directors of a publicly owned company and we have to define the objectives of our firm. (I think there is a somewhat different point of view in a private company than in a publicly owned one; we all know many private companies where the objectives may be to pay a certain amount of dividends for the family and get capital appreciation). One thing on which we would all agree is that we must make some profit or we will not get any bonuses, and the stockholders will be aroused. So one of our objectives is a level of earnings for the company. The question is: What kind of earnings? Or, what kind of profits? I think there are four possible answers: (1) growth of earnings; (2) level of earnings: what return on investment are we going to get?

---

* A special workshop to which participants were invited with the understanding that the proceedings would be recorded for possible use in this report.

(3) in a cyclical industry stability of earnings may be the dominant factor; finally, connected with each of the other three, there is earnings payout or dividend level. If we are to have some sort of earnings yardstick, which of these is the major measure against the objectives of the overall enterprise?

One workshop participant stated that his company's sole measure of performance against objectives is earnings. Two others said that, in their firms, return on investment is the yardstick. Mr. Granger replied:

I look at it quite differently, and this sometimes surprises people. But I think I can defend my stand. From the viewpoint of the financial community—which represents, in effect, the investing public—growth in earnings per common share is the really significant criterion. Here is the reason: there are about two dozen people in the United States who determine whether a public company is successful in the eyes of the investing community, and this has a great deal to do with the question of whether it is successful in terms of the management. These two dozen people are the chief analysts of the leading investment and brokerage firms on Wall Street. Their attitude is, "What have you done for me lately?" By that they mean, "Have your earnings per share been going up?" If earnings per share are rising the stock price probably has been going up, and there is the potential for an increase in dividends. Outspoken stockholders are not quite so hard as they otherwise might have been. And there is a chance that the management will get bonuses. The president is very happy. And this is what corporate life is all about: the company's growth of earnings per share.

This is not necessarily true in an operating division. A division manager's effect on earnings per share is limited. He is not ordinarily in a position to decide whether additional shares of stock will be issued, or whether funded debt will be used for leverage. For a division manager, then, return on investment is the key factor.

It may be asked whether growth in earnings per share is not almost the same thing as high return on investment. The answer is, "not necessarily." One of our clients in the electrical field had a consistently high return on investment. But the company's earnings per share were about $3, year in and year out, and while other stocks were going up, this firm's sold at about the same price as in the 1950's. Naturally, the stockholders and board were unhappy. And the analysts were saying: "Possibly the stock is a sound investment for dividend payouts, but it is not the sort of thing we can recommend to investors for growth or appreciation." In the last few years, however, the condition has been corrected. The company has not only a high return on investment; its earnings per share are going up. It had been accumulating a great deal of cash. This cash is now being used to bring in additional sources of earnings, so their total earnings are going up. The point I want to make is that the financial community is looking for future growth in earnings. Of course, a nice record of past growth is very often an indication of future growth.

Question: Wouldn't the relative importance of return on investment and earnings appreciation depend, to a large extent, on what the company is planning to do in the future? For instance, in a company which is acquisition-minded, you would be definitely concerned with stock appreciation for trading purposes. But a company which is not acquisition-minded would put much heavier emphasis on return on investment, wouldn't it, rather than earnings appreciation?

Granger: Take, as an example, United States Steel, for which I expect any sort of acquisition —in the United States, at least—is out of the question. No, I think growth in earnings per share is what the investment community is really looking for. This fact is going to affect the price of your stock, and if you've got stock options, it's going to affect your management. Standard and Poor's 425 industrials are showing an aggregate growth rate in earnings per share of about 4.5 percent a year. [See Exhibit 5.] If you're IBM or Xerox, you're doing two or three times that well; and a number of companies are doing better than this. If your earnings growth or your level of earnings has been low, your objective for the total enterprise should be to do at least as well. Return on investment in these 425 companies is running about 11 percent a year.

In this workshop session we are playing the role of the board of directors. It's plain that, by this yardstick, we should have $10 earnings per share a year by 1970 if we're going to be a successful company. What are we going to do about it? The dictionary says that an objective "is an aim or end of action." If so, there is a whole complex of objectives that probably we shall have to consider at the board of directors level. How to translate and transmit these objectives to the organization is the problem.

Many authors have addressed themselves to the same issue. Gordon Donaldson is one who emphasizes the importance of earnings per share and dividends as the stockholder's prime yardsticks for measuring a company's financial performance (11), as do Benjamin Graham and David L. Dodd in their classic book, *Security Analysis.*

As security analysts, Graham and Dodd of course include assets and capital structure as major elements in their scheme of evaluation. They also stress price-earnings ratio as a sound market test of past performance and future prospects:

A strong, successful, and promising company usually sells at a higher multiplier of current or average earnings than one that is less strong, less successful, and less promising. The chief factors that govern the average or characteristic price-earnings ratios for a given stock may be listed in the following order:

1. The *dividend* rate and record.
2. *Profitability*—rate of return on invested capital.
3. *Stability of past earnings.*
4. *Growth* of sales and earnings in the past.
5. Financial strength or credit standing.
6. Nature and prospects of the industry.
7. Competitive position and individual prospects of the company.
8. Quality of management.(12)

There is an impressive uniformity of opinion among representatives of the investment community as to the measures to be

(text continued on page 30)

EXHIBIT 5. *Profit Results in Industrial Companies*

EARNINGS PER
COMMON SHARE

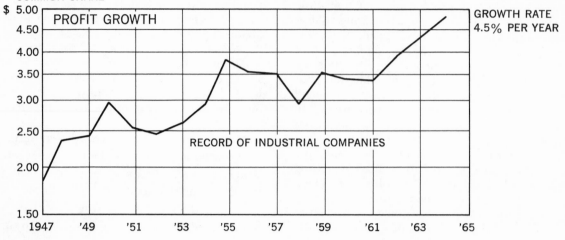

NET PROFIT ON
COMMON EQUITY

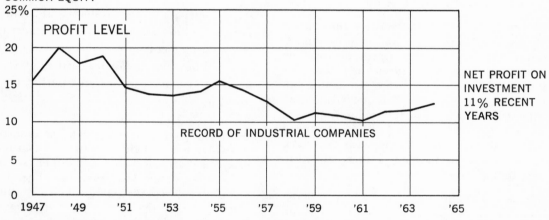

EARNINGS PER
COMMON SHARE

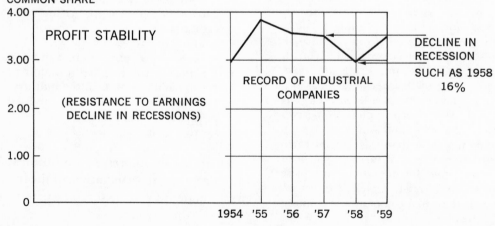

EXHIBIT 5a. *Earnings and Dividends per Share of Industrial Companies*

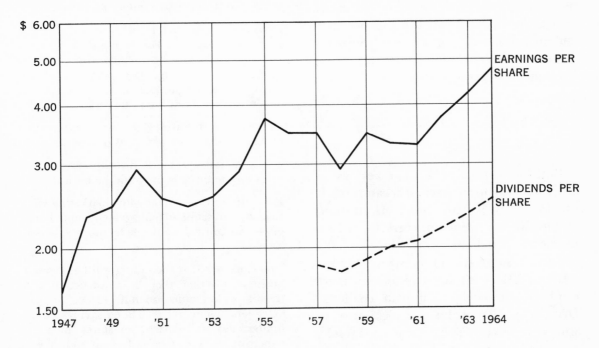

EXHIBIT 5b. *Dividends as a Percent of Earnings per Share*

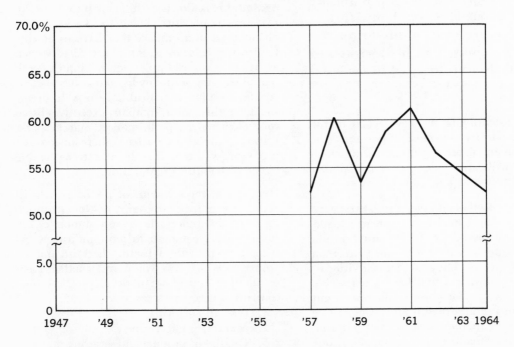

SOURCE: Chart published by William E. Hill & Company, Inc., 1965.

(text continued from page 27)

used in appraising a company. Foremost among these measures are earnings per share and growth in earnings per share. Supporting measures are trend of sales, return on investment, and equity.

APPROACHES OF SELECTED INDUSTRIAL COMPANIES

But, more specifically, what key results areas have companies set to measure their progress? This is Peter Drucker's position: "Objectives are needed in every area where performance and results directly and vitally affect the survival and prosperity of the business."(13) With this point of view there can be no quarrel. Nor will many challenge Drucker's listing of the ". . . eight areas in which objectives of performance and results have to be set: market standing; innovation; productivity; physical and financial resources; profitability; manager performance and development; worker performance and attitude; public responsibility."(14)

Richard F. Neuschel, a director of McKinsey & Company, Inc., has also stressed the critical elements involved in successful planning and control.

This step [identifying the key factors of the business] is clearly the most important. The imagination and depth of thinking with which it is done will largely determine the quality of the whole planning-and-control process.

The first step itself breaks down into two parts: *First*, isolate the critical factors on which success of the business depends. For any business these will ordinarily consist of not more than four to six factors. They are the activities or aspects of the business that have a major impact, not only on short-term profit results but also on long-term growth and competitive strength. They are the factors of such continuing significance that the breakdown of any one of them for a sustained period would, at best,

impair earnings and industry position and, at worst, put the company out of business.

Obviously, these factors will vary widely from industry to industry. For example, in the automotive industry they include (but are not limited to) car styling, maintenance of a hard-hitting dealer organization, and achievement of competitive manufacturing costs.

In the chemical business the list would include development of new products or new uses.

For a major appliance distributor, effective inventory management would be critical.

For a life insurance company, marketing effectiveness, investment management, and home-office cost control would be among the keys to success.

The story is much the same for other types of business, whether they be construction contractors, electronics manufacturers, plastics extruders, commercial airlines, savings banks, lumber dealers, department stores, or newspaper publishers. For each such industry, a relatively small number of key factors controls company success. For no two industries will this list of factors be exactly the same.

Second, break down each factor into its profit-making components. These are the important elements of performance that have to be controlled individually to insure satisfactory overall results. For example, one consumer goods manufacturing company listed marketing effectiveness as a factor critical to success. In breaking down this factor, company executives listed four elements of performance: market penetration (number of outlets), share of market, profitability of the mix sold, and strengthening of the distributor organization.

Here again, the elements of performance will vary from company to company. Notwithstanding these differences, there are a number of key control areas common to most industries. As such, they provide a useful checklist and an approach which any company, whether large or small, can follow in developing its own controls. These key areas are:
1. Overall performance.
2. Marketing effectiveness.
3. Quality of product and service.
4. Cost performance.

5. Financial position.
6. Creativity.
7. Personnel resources.
8. Payout from investment.(15)

General Electric Company

General Electric Company was an early contributor to increased sophistication in identifying long-term objectives and measuring progress toward achieving them. Robert W. Lewis, who at the time of the company's original research into this aspect of planning and control was manager, measurement services, accounting services division, has outlined General Electric's approach:

In approaching the problem of developing operational measurements, we asked ourselves this question: What are the specific areas for which measurements should be designed, bearing in mind that sound measurements of overall performance require a proper balance among the various functions and among the aspects (planning, organizing, for example) of managing? In seeking an answer to this question, a careful analysis was made of the nature and purposes of the basic kinds of work performed by each function, with the purpose of singling out those functional objectives which were of sufficient importance to the welfare of the business as a whole as to be termed "key result areas."

To check whether a tentative area was sufficiently basic to qualify as a key result area, this test question was applied:

"Will continued failure in this area prevent the attainment of management's responsibility for advancing General Electric as a leader in a strong competitive economy, even though results in all other key result areas are good?"

The result of this evaluation produced the following eight key result areas:
1. Profitability.
2. Market position.
3. Productivity.
4. Product leadership.
5. Personnel development.
6. Employee attitudes.
7. Public responsibility.
8. Balance between short-range and long-range goals.

Key Result Area Number 8 is, of course, essentially different in nature from the other seven. The decision to segregate it initially as a separate area is simply to recognize that its significance is so basic that we prefer to risk overemphasis rather than underemphasis.(16)

A Chemical Company

One large chemical company undertook intensive study to prepare for launching its program of management by objectives. One result of the research was the identification of the seven key results areas to be used in the firm's profit centers and the six to be used in the service and support departments. The executive responsible for the company's management by objectives program listed the areas as follows: (In each of the two lists, the most important area has first place.)

Profit Centers
1. Profitability and growth.
2. Market penetration.
3. Innovation.
4. Productivity improvement.
5. Physical and financial resources.
6. Personnel—attitude, development, resources.
7. Public responsibility.

Service and Support Departments
1. Contribution to profitability.
2. Innovation (adapting or creating within our department).
3. Productivity improvement (own function).
4. Physical and financial resources.
5. Personnel—attitude, development, resources.
6. Public responsibility.

The sum of the consideration of these key areas is the point of departure for setting shorter-term objectives.

The Boeing Company, Aerospace Group, Electronics Operations

In a memorandum setting forth the objectives of electronics operations of the aerospace group, The Boeing Company, John W. Maillet, manager, stated: "The first order of business for each member of management is to study this [planning guide] and then make certain that his personal objectives, plans, and efforts will support it to the fullest possible extent." The managers' efforts support five key results areas:

Operating Continuity. The maintenance of a capability sufficient to meet customer commitments. . . .

Personnel Development. The growth of people toward their full potential. . . .

Technical Excellence. The availability of the very latest resources in skill, knowledge, and facilities, at high enough levels for us to compete successfully as a space-age electronics manufacturer. . . .

Cost Effectiveness. Building a product of the required quality and reliability with less expenditure. . . .

Marketing. Our program for increasing electronics hardware sales.(17)

Westinghouse Air Brake Company

Rear Admiral Charles H. Smith, USN (retired), vice president and special assistant to the president of Westinghouse Air Brake Company, has summarized his firm's approach to management by objectives. Concerning the company's key results areas he wrote as follows:

If profitability is our primary objective, how do we know precisely what to accomplish, and how do we go about achieving it? In this company, we say that we will have accomplished our profitability objective if each profit-center attains and maintains a ____ percent return (exact figure deliberately omitted) on invested capital. With this objective always known, how do we assure that all the elements vital to profitability are accounted for? Our analysis led us to the decision that there are seven profitability result areas: (1) market position, (2) productivity, (3) innovation, (4) resources, (5) manpower development, (6) employee attitude, and (7) public responsibility.

Profitability is what we want, but it cannot be achieved unless we formulate and achieve objectives in each of the seven result areas. These—plus profitability—give us the eight vital words or terms. . . .

Market position—your relative status in the marketplace.

Productivity—your relative proficiency in use of resources to satisfy customer wants.

Innovation—your planned development of new products, services, or methods.

Resources—your acquisition, protection, conservation, and development of things needed.

Manpower development—your programs to increase individual or group capacity.

Employee attitude—your state of morale and discipline among the people under your supervision.

Public responsibility—the degree to which you assist and encourage your employees to participate in an enlightened manner in constructive civic, institutional, and governmental activities.

Our philosophy is that profitability is the total gain/loss resulting from success or failure to establish and to achieve optimum objectives in each of these profitability result areas; failure will result if any one is neglected over a sufficiently long period of time, and management is paid for exercising the judgment necessary to insure that available resources are properly allocated to the accomplishment of short-range and long-range objectives.(18)

These are the key long-term objectives that serve as guides to companies in their long-term planning and short-term objective setting. Among the organizations consulted in the course of this research, little variation in key results areas was observed. The early work of General Electric Company and of Peter Drucker has influenced most of the companies which have been concerned with long-term planning and objective setting. The soundness of this background is attested to by the number of companies which have adopted its substance, even though there have been minor modifications.

Planning for Accomplishment

Arthur H. Compton, physicist, educator, and Nobel Prize winner, has written in his book, *Atomic Quest*: "We couldn't afford elaborate equipment; so we had to think."(19) Setting objectives and planning to achieve them are "think" processes of management far more critical to success than is elaborate equipment or costly experimentation. Joseph C. Wilson, president of Xerox Corporation, has indicated the depth of his company's commitment to the "think" process in these words:

In 1964 we reached certain major decisions, as a result of several years of study and analysis, about the objectives of Xerox for the next 20 years. You realize, of course, that we cannot reveal to you just what these goals are, but we do emphasize that almost as much brains, energy, and money have gone into this long-range target setting as most companies of our size spend on their total research and development effort. We cannot overemphasize that at Xerox it is a way of life to be deeply concerned about the distant future. Hundreds of people throughout the company spend much time thinking of it. With great interest I read recently, in *The Economist*, an article about Japan's industrial growth. For the writer, Japan's success in outstripping all other countries in rate of economic growth since the war was at least in part due to the fact that throughout industry and government the nation's leaders were planning for growth and were solidly convinced of its necessity. It was no ivory-tower staff which thought of the future. It was Japan's leaders—who had the jobs to do. This is an attitude which has been nurtured at Xerox like the rare and tender plant it is.(20)

The unanimity of opinion that long-term planning and short-term objective setting must be closely related at all levels of management is impressive. Examples from a representative sample of respondents emphasize this agreement:

Our objectives by profit centers—and by the company as a whole—are integrated with long-term plans in the sense that where present performance is not up to standard, we try to make changes, either internally or by acquisition, in order to improve the situation. [W. A. Harshaw, president, The Harshaw Chemical Company]

We have a five-year plan. This plan is based upon broad objectives, and funnels into specific objectives. Short-term objectives year by year are integrated with those of the long-range plan, and these objectives in turn are made functional through their fragmentation to functional units. [Robert O. Barber, president, Univis, Inc.]

Objectives currently established are part of longer-term plans, and our efforts toward development of specific current objectives have brought about increased realization of the importance of more extensive long-range planning. [C. F. Schlueter, vice president-branch operations, Employers Mutuals of Wausau]

Objectives must be keyed to published institutional objectives and goals, which are in turn keyed to long-range plans. [Seeber C. Tarbell, director of personnel, Agway, Inc.]

Achievement of the target plan by an individual should result in a distinct improvement in performance of the organization unit as a whole and of that part he manages. Therefore, the target plan for an individual should be related to the near-term and long-range objectives of the unit and of the company.(21) [Westinghouse Electric Corporation's *Management Guide*]

This year, in preparation for our fiscal year beginning April 1, the operating division general managers and corporate department heads were asked to present their division or department objectives at the time of their financial budget reviews. Prior to the reviews, the broad objectives of the corporation were established and communicated to these people. The objectives then, for each of the divisions and departments, were a translation of the corporate objectives as they affected each of these units. At the financial review the various unit objectives were discussed and approved. These then became the agreed-upon objectives for that unit's management team, and in certain instances were further translated into individual objectives. [G. T. Canatsey, director of management development, Pet Milk Company]

Each year, the manager of each corporate staff department and the president of each subsidiary company make a formal presentation before the corporate executive committee. This presentation consists of a forecast of objectives and plans for the coming year. It will not only outline activities for the year to come, but will [also] relate them to previous years. It will bring out any significant trends; point out any unusual variations from normal; bring out any large expenditure requirements and any significant changes in manpower needs. It will also include a comparison of actual accomplishments versus forecasted objectives of the year just past. In summary, the program will be expressed in terms of capital requirements and budgets, along with principal expense categories, and will be presented to the executive committee for endorsement.

In addition and as an integral part of the presentation, there is a review of the use and development of management manpower. This is included to assure that there exists a planned program of replacement for each key job in the organization.

The presentation is more in the nature of a forecast and appraisal of objectives, both as to profits and to manpower, than a formal budget report. [O. N. Miller, president, Standard Oil Company of California]

Our procedures are not firmly integrated in this specific area. However, the specific objectives at the highest level of our corporation have been keyed to the corporation's five- and ten-year objectives, and this approach is followed through each echelon of management at a successively diminishing degree, with first-level

management concerned only with the year-to-year goals. [A. B. Foy, vice president of industrial relations, Transcon Lines]

The weight of support goes to a management process that begins at the top of the organization—the level where broad strategy and long-term plans are made—and from there proceeds to identify the more specific objectives which must be achieved if the strategy is to succeed.

There are dissenters to this practice, however. In most cases they dissent on "practical" grounds. Charles Granger's position is expressed in these words: ". . . while it would be ideal to follow the theoretically best pattern—that is, starting at the top and working down—when you are launching a management by objectives program you often can't do this. You start by setting objectives wherever you can—in the middle, at the top, at the bottom, or a combination of these. The important thing is to get started." Obviously, this is a *tactical* dissent; Granger would follow the theoretically ideal pattern whenever possible.

John J. Simpkins, manager of management services, Metropolitan Life Insurance Company, also suggests that the only practical approach to orienting management effort around objectives is to begin at whatever level and in whatever function it is possible, and thereafter let the success of the effort sell the orientation into other parts of the company. This is the way he has been working in his company. Here again, however, he admits that it would be ideal if the program was launched and supported by top management.

There seems to be little basic disagreement with the ideal; the dissenters do not deny that the top, down approach is preferable; they only suggest an alternative to be used when this approach is not feasible.

Agreement is general that when long-term

plans and objectives exist and have been stated formally, short-term plans and objectives must be consistent with them. L. A. Carey tells a dramatic story of what happened at Continental Can Company, Inc. when management implemented its long-term planning program:

The best long-range plan is one which establishes a broad, flexible objective which can serve as a guideline for subordinate plans and which is not likely to become obsolete as a result of rapidly changing technology. The classic example, of course, is the buggy-whip manufacturer who set his goal to become a supplier of transportation equipment.

Most long-range plans must be more specific than this, of course, but if they are to be truly long-range they cannot be too precise. They must set an objective to be reached, but if they are to have the greatest chance for success, they must allow a reasonable amount of latitude in the precise means and timing. With the ultimate objective clearly defined, you are far less likely to be deflected by short-term obstacles or setbacks.

. . . as the result of careful appraisal of our long-term future as a producer of metal containers, our management determined to undertake a fundamental reorientation of our company's sales objectives. We would no longer be only a leading supplier of cans—we would become a supplier of the broadest line of packaging products available anywhere in the world. Not content with this generalized objective, General Clay, who was then our relatively new chairman of the board, announced at a management meeting in 1953 that our goal was to pass the $1 billion mark in sales in five years. Since our sales the previous year had amounted to barely half that figure after 50 years of steady growth, the announcement of this goal was received with great skepticism.

We soon learned, however, that the two objectives were based on a realistic plan and that both of them—diversification of our product line to encompass all forms of packaging and development of volume at an accelerated rate—

would be pursued with an absolute single-mindedness of purpose.

The thinking of everyone in the organization had to go through a re-education process, and in many cases a completely new approach to our business was dictated. We could no longer, as a company, approach every product with the question, "How can it be put in a can?" Instead we had to learn to ask, "How can we best package it?" This produced a mild case of corporate schizophrenia in some instances and required a firm adherence to the basic concept, on the part of top management, in the face of frequent conflicts among the burgeoning product divisions.

Little time was lost in setting the company out on the new course which had been charted for it. In what—in retrospect—seems like an astonishingly short time, we diversified into flexible packaging, glass containers, closures, paper packaging of all types, and, most recently, plastic bottles. Much of this was accomplished through mergers. But a broadening of product lines from within was also undertaken with considerable vigor to close the gaps between the operations which were being acquired. We soon learned that it was much easier to tell our top management why we should add a new product or enter a new market than it was to justify passing it by. If it was a package, it was our responsibility.

The two goals which were set for the company back in 1952 were met ahead of schedule. By 1957 we were major suppliers of virtually every type of package. And our sales passed the $1 billion mark in 1956—only four years after the decision to expand was made. The important point I want to make here is just this: we achieved these goals only because we established them as our primary objectives years ago and then determined the actions which would be necessary. We would never have gotten there as the result of normal market or industry development. Of course, the $1 billion goal became obsolete the day it was passed, but the more fundamental objective of being the leading supplier of the broadest line of packaging in the world is one we must go on achieving year after year. It is in the nature of a star by which we can chart our course and on which we can base our shorter-range plans indefinitely.(22)

NOTES TO CHAPTER 3

1. Rader, Louis T., "Roadblocks to Progress in the Management Sciences and Operations Research," *Management Science*, February 1965, p. C-4.
2. "The Shape and Character of Xerox," an address by Joseph C. Wilson, president, Xerox Corporation, before The Security Analysts of San Francisco, January 28, 1965, pp. 19-20.
3. *1965 Planning Guide*, Electronics Division, The Boeing Company.
4. Thompson, Stewart, *Management Creeds and Philosophies*, Research Study No. 32, American Management Association, 1958, p. 10.
5. *Ibid.*, p. 9.
6. *Ibid.*, p. 100.
7. *Ibid.*, p. 127.
8. "Professional Management in General Electric," *General Electric's Organization*, Book Two, General Electric Company, New York, 1955, p. 94.
9. *Ibid.*
10. *Ibid.*, p. 5.
11. Donaldson, Gordon, "Financial Goals: Management vs. Stockholders," *Harvard Business Review*, May-June 1963, p. 121.
12. Graham, B. J., and D. L. Dodd, *Security Analysis,* 3rd. ed., McGraw-Hill Book Co., Inc., 1951, p. 204.
13. Drucker, Peter, *The Practice of Management*, Harper & Bros., 1954, p. 63.
14. *Ibid.*
15. Neuschel, Richard, "Key Facts Mean Better Profits," *Nation's Business*, March 1957.
16. "Planning, Managing and Measuring the Business: A Case Study of Management Planning and Control at General Electric Company," Series II, Business Planning and Control. Report No. 3, Controllership Foundation, Inc., New York, 1955, pp. 30-31.
17. *1965 Planning Guide, op. cit.*, p. 2.
18. Smith, Charles H., "Management by Objectives as a Communication Device," In *Superior-Subordinate Communication in Management*, Research Study No. 52, American Management Association, 1961, p. 93.
19. Compton, Arthur H., *Atomic Quest*, Oxford University Press, Inc., New York, 1956.
20. *The Shape and Character of Xerox, op. cit.,* pp. 10-11.
21. "Management Performance Objectives," Management Guide GM-7 (revised), March 1963, Westinghouse Electric Corporation, Pittsburgh, p. 2.
22. Carey, L. A., "Setting Long-Range Sales Objectives in a Large Corporation," *Budgeting*, March 1965, pp. 11-12.

4. From Corporate to Individual Goals

THE COURSE THAT A BROAD company objectives program takes is determined by top management—usually, the chief executive and his staff and the board of directors. Before they can draw up the program, however, they must have all the information there is to be had on the essential factors: economic trends in the country and the company's industry; market research reports and forecasts that point to the position of present and potential products; the competition; the company's history (profit performance and operating costs); and evaluations of the management team. Once all these facts have been collected and interpreted, management is ready to formulate the overall corporate program from which departmental and individual objectives are derived.

In the majority of instances, a *company's* objectives are first formulated as part of its long-term plan. *Job* objectives are the standards for the job duties involved during the period for which the objectives are set.

Generally, objectives are considered informally at one or two subordinate levels so that higher management can make sure the objectives are feasible as well as appropriate and challenging. The objectives are stated formally only after this informal review.

There is a typical cycle in developing and communicating objectives and their results. It may be thought of as an intermeshing series of circular flows of information between and among levels and functions of the organization. The sequence is commonly from higher to lower levels and from marketing to research and engineering, manufacturing, personnel, finance, and from each to control.

Objectives usually owe their origin to plans. And, as previously noted, objectives become standards of performance for a specified period. But there are other standards of performance which are prepared to continue in force until changed circumstances require changed standards. They are commonly cast in a form that suggests relative permanence. These standards of performance, that are in effect an effort to put a floor under performance and that tend to emphasize control, are usually derived from job descriptions which spring from organization plans.

Standards of performance are usually prepared by job incumbents together with their supervisors. In every case, standards become official only after they receive the supervisor's approval, and often the approval of the next higher level of management is also required. The standards are frequently published as a section of, or supplement to, the job description.

In a fundamental sense, there is an adequate foundation for standards of performance only when a sound job of organization planning has been done.

FEEDBACK

Essential to the use of objectives and standards is a system to report back, for purposes of comparison, the results of performance. This is feedback.

Most systems require that the feedback go first to the job incumbent and next to his supervisor. The preferred approach is to have the man prepare a report, based on the feedback, for his supervisor; this gives him an opportunity to comment on variances and suggest changes in the program. Alternatively, the supervisor may receive a concurrent report and may then request analytical comment from the man. In any event, the results of performance are always fed back to the interested managers, who communicate with each other afterward if action will be required.

REVIEW AND REVISION

"Feedback" is one key word; "judgment" is another. By judging the factors involved in producing the variances between objectives (or standards) and their results, the manager decides whether effort should be increased within the existing framework or whether the objectives or standards should be changed. In most cases this matter will be decided by the man and his supervisor. It is usually done at least once a year for the man's whole job; as special problems arise, however, appropriate action is taken at the time. *All* objectives and standards are thus reviewed once a year, and *some* are reviewed

when results suggest that these are either too demanding or not demanding enough.

PARTICIPATION AND COMMUNICATION

The emphasis, from the very beginning, is on the participation of all to whom the objectives and standards are applicable. The participation of the man *and* his boss in setting, reviewing, and revising objectives and standards is all-important. The relative influence that either will have on the product of their engagement will depend on, among other factors: the supervisor's philosophy of management; the subordinate's experience and competence; and the economic health of the organization. How many other managers, at higher or lower levels in the organization or in other functions, become involved seems to depend on the company's sophistication in using the techniques and on its aggressiveness: the more sophisticated enlist the participation of more managers for each manager's job, and the more aggressive emphasize better-directed effort through better-shared knowledge.

About participation there is a notable consensus among the companies which aided in this research, and it may be expressed in this way: "Participation tends to increase commitment; commitment tends to heighten motivation; motivation which is job-oriented tends to make managers work harder and more productively; and harder and more productive work by managers tends to enhance the company's prosperity; therefore, participation is good."

Communication is another "why" of objectives and standards of performance. Almost all of those who took part in the research for this report emphasized communication's value. The importance of communication is recognized in all aspects of the effort; the plan for completing each step is designed to increase the effectiveness of the communication—to put it another way, "the complete and timely transmission of valid information." The participation of the man-supervisor unit in all phases of the objectives and standards activity is designed, in part, to produce effective information exchange. Meetings of groups of job incumbents, of managers of a number of functions, and of representatives of different organization levels are efforts to heighten the communication value of what is being done. Similar efforts are shown in the demonstrated emphasis on *written* statements of objectives and standards which are provided for all whose jobs are thus formally set down; the attention given to the development and use of an effective reporting system; and the requirement for scheduled reviews and discussions by the man with his supervisor.

The specific procedures vary from the highly informal to the closely structured. Some companies communicate these matters generally by word-of-mouth and put in writing only decisions and progress. Others use written statements which are very detailed in specifying what will be done, how, when, why, and by whom; preprinted forms are usually prepared for use in this approach. Still other companies employ procedures which fall between these two extremes.

The theory of progressing from the broad to the specific objective is direct and simple. How is it done in practice? Let us consider the experience of a few of the participating companies.

Otter Tail Power Company

This company's practice illustrates what may be considered an ideal approach. The company first reviewed past history and present strengths. It then formulated future objectives from which were derived, by major activities and functions, continuing and short-term objectives. Albert V. Hartl, president, is an enthusiastic user of objectives and performance standards for individual jobs. In his own words:

Company objectives have been prepared to provide a broad outline to serve as a guide for more specific objectives developed in various functional areas within the company. Annually, each functional area develops and restates its objectives, which, upon attainment, insures that its responsibilities are being met and adequate contributions are being made toward overall company goals. Likewise, development of yearly objectives is being encouraged at most management levels in the company, including company officers, major department heads, division managers, and district managers.

In 1962, as a result of a review of its history and the factors likely to influence the course of its future development, the company issued a statement of corporate objectives over the signature of the president. Following an introductory section which summarized the general factors and assumptions considered in formulating the company's broad objectives, this formal statement continued:

. . . reflection on these factors, favorable and adverse, would indicate that the company should set the following general objectives, which each department must implement by its shorter-range specific goals.

Corporate. Otter Tail Power Company's primary objective is to conduct a profitable business. The level of profitability should be equal to the industry average. We will conduct our affairs so as to be considered the dominant progressive utility in our general area. To that end, we dedicate ourselves to growth, not only internally but by purchase, acquisition, or merger with other power suppliers.

Power Supply. Study and evaluate the many sources and methods of obtaining our future power needs, to the end that the method (or methods) producing the greatest profitability and assurance of continued corporate identity is developed.

Operating. Practices and techniques in all departments shall be under such constant scrutiny and evolvement as to produce a continuous record of more efficient usage of tools and more effective utilization of man-hours.

Sales. Load growth of Otter Tail Power Company should be at least one-tenth of 1 percent above the national average. This is to be effected in part by innovation in the usage of our product or our facilities.

Control. Development of better interpretative techniques, to the end that management knows "why" at the same time it knows "what."

Rates. Immediate development of promotional rates, especially in commercial areas, that can be announced as rate reductions as soon as earnings and public relations conditions permit.

Personnel. Provide a productive and satisfying work environment for employees, offering career opportunities for personal development and advancement. Completion of personnel inventory and plan of succession at all management levels. Actual implementation of plan to shift junior executives to other jobs as an educational and observational technique. Broadening of general employee education, both as to company work and company problems.

Public Relations. Conduct our affairs and ourselves so as to assure favorable acceptance of Otter Tail Power Company from our employees, customers, investors, the industry, and the public at large. The full participation of all employees in the economic and political life of our service area is declared an intermediate goal. "No new vote on municipal ownership" and "no franchise unrenewed for more than six months" are declared as specific objectives.

President Hartl concluded with an expression of expectation that his executives would immediately begin to formulate short-term objectives for their own functions, using this memorandum as a guide.

To the best of my knowledge, this memorandum is the first effort of its type for our company. I expect that it will be added to, improved, modified, and otherwise changed from time to time. It is offered as a crude starting-point from which each of you will immediately

develop your "short-term" specific objectives and discuss with me "long-range" goals, to the end that this will be a living memorandum guiding the detail of each segment of Otter Tail Power Company.

One set of departmental objectives drawn up in response to this directive is recorded here. R. M. Bigwood, personnel manager, developed them for his department.

Long-Range and Continuing Objectives
1. Maintaining good relations between labor and management.
2. Strengthening the management role and view of foremen (who supervise others) and service representatives (who work with our public).
3. Evolving techniques and devices for keeping the employee educated and informed.
4. Maintenance of a management manpower plan which will permit looking ahead with assurance.

Short-Range Objectives (One Year)
1. To develop a more thoroughgoing orientation and indoctrination program for new employees; "Welcome to Otter Tail Family" Handbook.
2. To develop a manual containing organization charts as a learning and informational aid.
3. To implement the retirement preparation program by planning personal visits with those within five years of retirement.
4. To continue with personnel research and evaluation.
5. To continue with promotion of development of formal standards of performance in management and management-related jobs.
6. To institute a reading improvement program.
7. To encourage and insure a critical look at each promotional opportunity as it occurs to be sure that full consideration is given to the policy of promotion from within, while at the same time insuring that needed training areas or entry jobs for the new college-trained person are not being closed out and that adequate professionally trained talent is being brought into the organization.

8. To work with other departments in the development of a workable plan for exposing the junior executive to a more thoroughgoing management scrutiny. Temporary job shifts, special project assignments, and like techniques will be involved.

9. To develop display aids and techniques for use during recruiting efforts at educational institutions, which will do a more professional job of highlighting the company.

10. To continue with Group Ten Project participation, and see to it that maximum use is made of project statistics in evaluating personnel staffing and needs.

11. To follow through on a review of the more pertinent concepts set out in the customer relations program, through a one-day contact in each of the districts.

12. To undertake the U.S. Chamber of Commerce discussion series "Freedom Vs. Communism" for such employee groups as can be developed. Approach would be patterned after practical politics course, and it is planned to have both early morning and evening groups.

13. To develop during the year at least one new and different approach to general employee education and information.

14. To have Annual Meeting material developed by July 1.

15. To have a supervisor of employee services recruited for department no later than April 1.

Diamond Alkali Company

Diamond Alkali has been using objectives in its management process for over six years, according to Glenn H. Varney, manager of recruiting and development. Here again, the emphasis is on the systematic development and communication of objectives from the top of the organization down through all levels. While there are problems in the application of the process, results have been good enough to permit more aggressive work on the development and application of standards of performance.

The company emphasizes the close tie be-tween corporate long-term objectives and unit and individual objectives. As a means of making this relationship understood, Varney has found a simple diagram helpful (Exhibit 6). Each such individual objective is tested to ascertain that it contributes to the objectives of the unit. Next, unit objectives are tested in terms of department and division objectives, which are rationalized in their turn with corporate objectives.

How the time element is shown in review and control is illustrated in this schedule:

Objective: Improve performance review program results by November 1.

Phase No. 1: Determine problem areas, and submit to director of employee relations a plan for corrective action by June 1.

Phase No. 2: If plan is approved, initiate plan and complete by November 1.

DIFFICULTIES ENCOUNTERED

The process of deriving short-term objectives from broader plans is clear in concept but often difficult in fact. Many participants in this research mentioned problems they had encountered. Gerry E. Morse, vice president, Honeywell, Inc., is one who set forth his company's difficulties concisely but covered them all:

The major difficulty we have encountered is to pick out the important, key, measurable elements in each assignment so that objectives can be stated in a way that does most effectively focus a man's ability and effort on the core elements of his assignments, yet are expressible in sufficiently objective measurable terms so that both the man and his superior see his progress. . . . Because some of the less tangible requirements, such as cooperation with other units, the maintenance of high morale, or the proper attention to long-range requirements, are more difficult to reflect in measurable, one-year terms, we are still seeking a better way to reflect them in an executive's objectives.

EXHIBIT 6. *The Relation of Objectives on Four Company Levels*

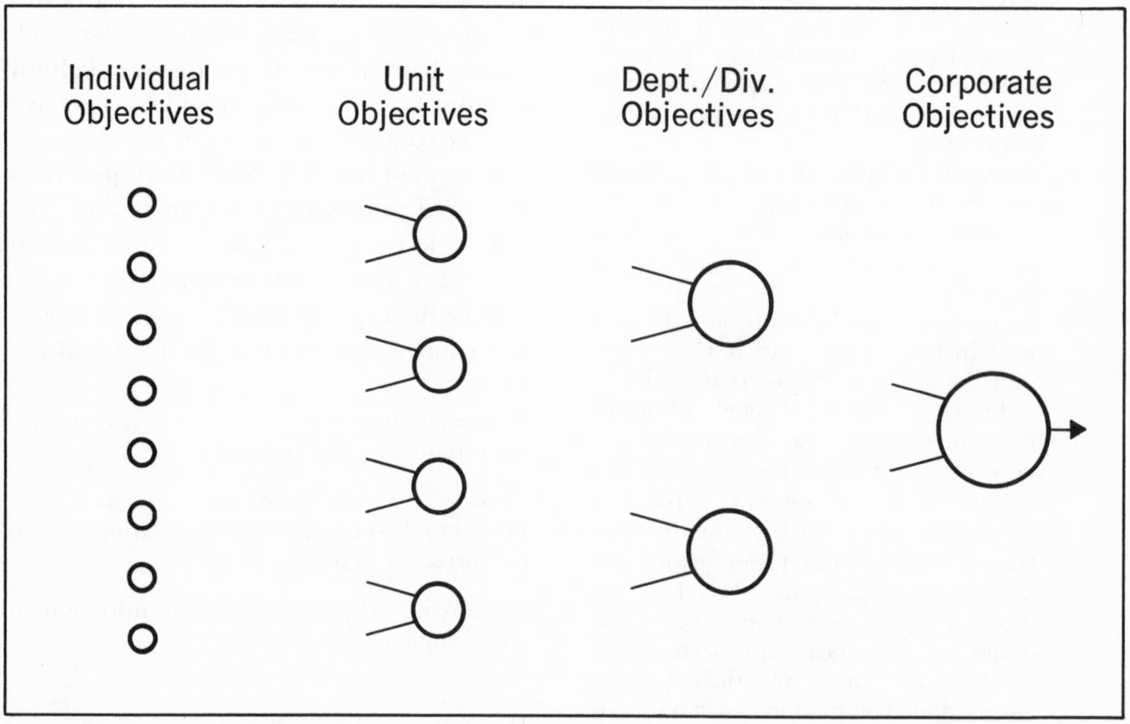

Setting objectives for staff positions is a frequently mentioned trouble spot. To George C. Delp, president of New Holland Machine Company (a division of Sperry Rand Corporation), the major difficulty encountered has largely been "the problem of developing measurable objectives in the case of staff positions and areas of work where operations are substantially affected by outside influences. Obviously, the 'management by objectives' approach can be expected to be less effective in these areas than where a manager has a complete operation under his control."

GUIDELINES FOR ORIENTATION

Given the importance of setting high objectives, and the accompanying difficulties we have observed, what criteria do companies choose to guide them in drawing up challenging objectives? The general policy

and procedure on management by objectives of New Holland Machine Company gives this advice:

Objectives do not normally include routine tasks for which a manager or supervisor is accountable. Instead, the objectives should be oriented toward goals of a creative nature, or special or breakthrough type of activities or innovations resulting from new technologies or new approaches to problems. Also, objectives may be oriented toward improved sales or profits, cost reduction, completion of specific projects, improvement in service, etc. In all instances, it is desirable to establish a statistical or monetary value against which results can be measured.(1)

C. J. Gauthier, executive vice president, Northern Illinois Gas Company, stresses the quantitative approach: "To the extent possible, our goals are specifically quantified (percent improvement, dollar per unit, earnings per share, etc.). The goals relate to individual jobs, departments, divisions, and the company as a whole."

In an article in *Business Horizons* Dale D. McConkey, administrative vice president, United Fruit Company, has told what, in his experience, is most important in objective setting. First, he sets the criteria the superior uses in reviewing the objectives submitted to him:

1. Does the objective represent a sufficient task for the manager during the measuring period?
2. Is the objective a practical and attainable one?
3. Is the objective clearly stated in terms of the task? The measuring period? The method of measuring to be used?
4. Is the objective compatible with the company's plans for the period?(2)

How Many Objectives?

Later in the same article, McConkey goes on record as believing that the nature of the job should dictate the number of objectives that should be set for the job, and the weight given to each objective.

Certain theoreticians advocate that only a limited number of objectives should be set for any manager, and that a responsibility should not be included as an objective unless it constitutes a certain minimum percentage of the time required for the overall task for the period. Thus, if a particular responsibility constitutes only 5 percent of the total task for the period, it should not be included because (1) it might detract from the more important objectives, or (2) several small items might be substituted for a few more important ones.

I quarrel with this school of thought on two counts. First, in applying measurement by objectives to all levels of management, one cannot follow any standard format; the number and percentage weights of objectives must be dictated by the nature of the job. Second, the time required to accomplish a particular objective is not indicative of the importance or contribution of that objective to the company; that is,

a task requiring only 10 percent of an executive's time may be worth infinitely more to the company than one requiring 30 percent of his time.(3)

As we have seen, the most suitable number of objectives is a point on which reasonable men disagree. Part of the disagreement seems to spring from failing to consider, at the very outset, whether the objectives to be developed are for a job, a department, or a business. To cover an entire business may require eight objectives from one point of view, or 40 from another. But it seems that the eight objectives covering key results areas are more appropriate at the level of the business, while the 40, when divided among the five usual major business functions, give eight objectives to each function. This suggests that another part of the disagreement originates from lack of accord on the appropriate degree of generality with which objectives should be set.

Many authorities on management—whether writers or company managers—have definite ideas on this subject. One author, Edward C. Schleh, says: "As a working rule, *no position should have more than two to five objectives.*"(4) But Clyde O. DeLong, former assistant (now retired) to the president, The B.F. Goodrich Company, states that Goodrich usually sets six to ten job objectives.

Among companies, such variations in approach to objective setting are frequently found. A partial explanation may lie in the scope of their objectives. One large chemical company sets objectives for its profit centers and major departments for five years, a longer than usual term, and these are its instructions for top management's use in stating and presenting objectives:

The number of objectives for each key result area should be kept to a minimum. One or two objectives in each area generally should be sufficient and will more readily be retained in people's minds.

Objectives in each of the first five key result areas should be expressed in quantitative terms; that is, in numeric terms including ratios and percentages. Objectives in the other key result areas (personnel and public responsibility) may, at present, need to be expressed in qualitative terms where judgment will be a major factor in evaluation.

The lack of current means of obtaining measurement data should not be considered as cause for elimination of a standard for an objective.

At middle and lower management in this company, many more and narrower objectives are set in order to attain the broad profit center objectives. The firm's subordinate objective program for two key result areas is reproduced in Exhibit 7.

And so the process seems to go: to the extent that there is a modal range in number of objectives, and assuming that the objectives have been set at the degree of generality appropriate to the organization level to which they are applied, their number will be from three to ten objectives for a set period, usually one year.

As debate continues on the proper number of objectives for a job, it is well to keep in mind the principle of "the vital few and the trivial many," expounded by J. M. Juran. This he calls "the Pareto Principle," after Vilfredo Pareto, the 19th century economist whose studies of personal wealth recognized that important resources are distributed unevenly. Juran applies the principle to the selection of objectives: there are "the vital few" which account for most of the worthwhile results, and "the trivial many" which have only a marginal influence.(5)

STAFF RESPONSIBILITY
CALLS FOR STAFF OBJECTIVES

Another problem frequently mentioned is setting objectives for staff. Progress is re-
ported, although few companies express full satisfaction with their results. RCA, for example, after successfully using objectives for line managers for many years, only recently has indicated some favorable results for staff positions. The present attitude is toward holding staff accountable for the line objectives to which they can contribute, on the assumption that staff is responsible for persuading the line to follow its advice.

Schleh has consistently faced up to this problem. He recommends that line and staff have joint responsibility for accomplishing the company's objectives, and has expressed this idea as follows:

This new theory holds that a man can and should be fully accountable for a result, even if he has only a partial influence on that result and several other people can either make or break the success of the project. This fulfills the company's original aim—to get adequate direction and drive toward its objectives—far more effectively than the old unique accountability methods.

Results, then, may be credited (or discredited) to two or three individuals. This violates another tradition: the basic accounting tenet of no more than 100 percent allocation of any charge. For example, a specific sale may result from the combined work of a salesman selling in a home office and a salesman selling in a branch plant. If the sale is consummated, both should presumably get full credit for the sale: 200 percent credit. It may never be known who contributed the most to the sale; but by giving full credit to both men, management will obtain a more coordinated sales effort than it would by measuring each person's contribution separately.

This approach is especially important for getting value from staff. If staff executives are measured by the final result achieved in the line, and both line and staff are given full credit for the result, more staff-line cooperation is obtained. It now becomes advantageous for both to cooperate fully. This, of course, leads to a different type of organizational setup for staff functions. Staff men are no longer put on a basis of simply advising, but are imbedded

EXHIBIT 7. *Five-Year Objectives for Two Key Result Areas in a Profit Center (A Large Chemical Company)*

Subordinate Objective and Program

KEY RESULT AREA: Market penetration.

OBJECTIVE: To increase our share of the XYZ chemical U.S. market from 10% in 19____ to 12% in 19____ (five-year period).

MEASUREMENT CRITERIA

$$\% \text{ of U.S. market} = \frac{\text{Sales by profit center}}{\substack{\text{Sales of chemicals to the XYZ industry} \\ \text{(as reported by XYZ trade association)}}}$$

SPECIFIC LONG-RANGE PROGRAM FOR REACHING OBJECTIVE

Marketing Plans for Increasing Our Share of Market with Present Products. We have analyzed our market, territory by territory, and will analyze it by principal customers. Special sales emphasis will be placed on all territories with less than 10% of the market share. This has shown the necessity for much greater sales effort in Arizona, Washington, and New England. We plan to obtain distributors to cover Arizona and Washington, but we will rearrange our sales territories in the New England area, perhaps adding one more sales representative. We expect the greatest growth of the market in New England, and we have a better freight position in this area. We are going to attempt to achieve 30% of the market in this area.

Marketing Plans for New Products and New Applications. The new product X, which it appears will be ready for commercialization two years from now, presents some very difficult marketing problems. Our market research studies have shown a critical need for the product, but its application is so radical that we must plan our approach very carefully. We have a team of sales, advertising, technical service, and research people working on marketing plans. We plan to test-market the product in Alabama and in the Chicago territories before going nationwide.

Supporting Projects

RESULT AREA: Market penetration.

Project Title: Arizona distributor.

Assigned to: Southwest district manager.

Assigned date: *Target Date:* (13 months from   *Completion Date:*
                              assigned date)

Project Goal: To obtain a satisfactory distributor or distributors to handle our complete line of products in the state of Arizona.

Results Obtained:

Project Title: Washington distributor.

EXHIBIT 7. (cont'd)

Assigned to: Northwest district manager.

Assigned Date: *Target Date:* (ten months from   *Completion Date:*
                                assigned date)

Project Goal: To obtain a satisfactory distributor or distributors to handle our complete line of products in the state of Washington.

Results Obtained:

Project Title: Realignment of New England sales territories.

Assigned to: Market research manager.

Assigned Date: *Target Date:* (six months from   *Completion Date:*
                                assigned date)

Project Goal: To develop at least two alternate territory plans for New England which can insure us at least 30% of the market.

Results Obtained:

Project Title: Product X marketing plans.

Assigned to: Sales manager.

Assigned Date: *Target Date:* (seven months from   *Completion Date:*
                                assigned date)

Project Goal: To develop at least two alternate marketing plans for new product X. Plans to include advertising, technical services, and sales approaches. To outline two test market plans. Include any necessary plans for additional personnel or retraining required.

Results Obtained:

Subordinate Objective and Program

KEY RESULT AREA: Productivity improvement.

OBJECTIVES

To increase the annual rate of the "profit improvement program" from $_____ in 19___ to $_____ in 19___ (five-year period).

To improve the ratio of sales to selling expense from 11.1 to 1 in 19___ to 12.9 to 1 in 19___ (five-year period).

MEASUREMENT CRITERIA: Statistically developed.

$$\text{Sales} \div \text{Selling Expense}$$

SPECIFIC LONG-RANGE PROGRAM FOR REACHING OBJECTIVE

Manufacturing

Studies presently under way indicate that savings of more than $300,000 per year can be achieved through increased automation of equipment in plant C and by increasing the compressor and refrigeration capacity, thereby increasing the capacity of this plant to 35 million pounds. This will permit the shutting down of the inefficient operations at our tanbark plant.

In addition studies will be made of our maintenance operations, supervisory staff, and plant administration areas. Particular attention will be given to improved methods of maintenance job order control. It is believed that, by planning our maintenance operations so as to work against a standard backlog of job orders, a reduction of about one-fourth in our maintenance force can be achieved.

Our ratio of supervisors to production workers appears high. Studies will be made to determine where reductions can be made. As part of this study, we plan to develop means to broaden the responsibility and increase the interest and challenge of these positions.

Selling

Increased productivity in our selling efforts will be achieved by holding additions to our staff to a minimum—perhaps one additional sales representative in the New England area and two additions to our technical service force for our line of Vical resins.

Rearrangement of our sales territories plus improvement in our call system will be the main means used to increase productivity.

---

in the actual operation itself. Consequently, not only do they become better accepted by the line because they are now accountable for line results; they take a more practical attitude when the measurement of their work is based on accomplishment in the line.(6)

It is becoming more common for staff managers to set objectives for which they will be accountable but for which the line organization will retain primary responsibility and almost total authority to commit the resources necessary for acceptable performance.

CHALLENGE AND MOTIVATION

David Ewing, author of *The Managerial Mind,* notes that the relationship between challenge and motivation is also closely bound to the sought-for forward thrust of objectives.

If members of a group want to avoid the mess and confusion of change, they can be "reasonable" about it. In order to avoid being disturbed, they can simply aspire to very modest goals. In order to spare themselves hurt feelings and failure, they can make it a point not to do anything unconventional. They can make neatness and tranquillity their objectives, and they can see that nothing upsets their pet schemes and prejudices.

The danger of continuous success, in other words, is that it tempts employees to forget that their real strength, in the last analysis, is their ability to respond through creative interaction to the ever changing needs of the world they serve.

There is a second and more important reason for fearing too smooth a record of success. The manager senses that no organization can have such a record if it is raising its sights high enough. Lack of failure is a sign of lack of aggressiveness. Unless he can somehow coax his department or enterprise to reach for a little more than it can surely grasp, and can deliberately drive it to taste frustration from time to time, he can never claim that he has done his utmost to help it learn and progress. He does not fear "pushing the luck" of an organization too far, "asking for too much" from a work group, or forcing a conflict into the open, simply because trouble and failure may result (although he must, of course, see a positive value to be gained).(7)

This insight is an old one, and it has been meaningful to many people in many different kinds of situations.

This attitude is consistent with a point made by William Holmes of Lever Brothers Company when he commented on the findings from his informal survey of the opinions of executive selection experts as to how the greatest improvement in executive performance will be obtained in the future.

. . . the consensus of experts was that better selection techniques contribute to improved performance. Estimates vary, but well-planned selection might contribute something on the order of 25 percent improvement over chance selection. Even greater opportunities for performance improvement seem to be in the field of motivation. It is plausible to assume that many managers are functioning at 50 percent of their potential. Think what a major contribution we could make by altering organization arrangements, leadership style, and management climate to increase the percent of realized manager potential. This should be an area of primary interest and concern for all of us.

Holmes believes that proper use of newly evolving management concepts (management by objectives, for example) offers real opportunity for breakthrough in manager performance.

To give a clearer understanding of the ways in which companies use objectives in the management process, the experiences of three firms which have used management by objectives extensively are reviewed here. The major part of these case studies is com-

posed of edited material from the transcript of the AMA research workshop.

Company Experience:
1. General Electric Company

The departments of General Electric have substantial autonomy in selecting their management procedures; varying approaches to management by objectives may, therefore, be found in this company. The essence of General Electric's approach is a close integration between business planning and work planning for each job. Clarence Gray, area personnel supervisor for the Large Jet Engine Department, described the procedure used in his department:

The corporate executive office approves the business charter for each of the product departments. The charter generally describes the product, the market area, and the scope of the business of that department. This method keeps the hundred or so product departments from competing overzealously with each other rather than with outside competitors. We receive policies and guidelines from the corporate level on organization, product selection, and financial reports and controls. I'm working at the department level, where the prime task is to take these managerial theories and policies and translate them into language that operating managers can use in getting their job done.

. . . In looking critically at what has been going on in the last several years, we concluded that there was an overemphasis on scorekeeping, and perhaps even on planning, and not enough concern on what happens during the game. Endless amounts of time can be spent in devising better performance standards and deciding where to put the checkmarks, with little real contribution to obtaining results for the business. As an example, we have had almost perfect coverage on appraisals and discussions. However, we couldn't say that this contributed significantly to the business results. Maybe this was time wasted. In looking critically at the managerial steps being taken, and in talking with a number of our general managers and those who report directly to them, we learned that they have great difficulty in describing what they themselves must do to make a business go. Each one has a considerably different impression. Yet we believe that if a team of managers in a product department is to be successful, they have to understand and follow the same managerial processes.

Our former approach to objectives and goals assumed a fairly static condition from the beginning to the end. This just wasn't realistic. While there is long lead time in the development of new engines, and there is long lead time in the manufacturing of an engine, we found that the business plan described at the beginning of the year invariably gets two or three major changes during the next 12 months. Our former system of appraisals was not flexible enough to get the new information coming from the top down; neither was the system flexible enough to take into account the working situations that the people at the working level were encountering. We had a system that was locked in place at "X day," against which everyone tended to try to perform and measure. At the end of a year, or at the end of a cycle, a rather academic discussion took place that had little or no reality as to what had really occurred in the business.

Also, there had been a tendency to do the goal setting or the selection of work, on a "bottom-up" basis, the assumption being that the "bottom" could make its own assumptions about the business and select the right things to emphasize. We found, however, that any given group of managers, even at high levels, make totally different assumptions from the same basic documents, and that their planning had serious gaps when viewed by a general manager. Also, there were extensive overlaps; so we concluded that total dependency on "bottom-up" planning wasn't going to produce what we wanted in terms of job performance at the working levels.

Our former system of appraising and trying to measure encouraged the idea that each manager was "an island unto himself," and that, while he might look sorrowfully at his peers, he really need not be much concerned with what was happening to them. We found that there was a belief that you could have several individual performers in an organizational element who were highly successful and rated so, while at the same time the organization's contribution to the business could be well below expectations. This failure to appreciate that there must be close correlation between the cumulative results of a group of people and the measures applied to that business component was a critical factor in our revised approach to measuring.

About three years ago, a new general manager was appointed for one large department in Cincinnati. With this new manager we had an opportunity to alter some of our past practices. (Sometimes, with new managers, you can approach old problems with new techniques.) About the same time, in other parts of the company, behavioral research studies were being run, especially at the plant in Lynn. These studies centered around the reaction to, and the effectiveness of, the whole appraisal concept, the reaction of both the manager and the man, and the impact of trying to relate appraisal to pay. We studied the results quite carefully, as well as other reports issued by the corporate staff on activities related to manager training, and decided that we would take a different tack than previously had been used . . .

With the new general manager our approach was one of looking critically at what managers need to know and need to do in order to improve the management of the business.

We asked: What are the essential pieces of work that every manager must do? What must he know in order to carry out this work? What are his working relationships with other managers? The business charter for the department is a point of departure. From that the general manager and his staff, on a group basis, determine the goals or areas of emphasis. Some of these goals will be two- or three-month types, some will run a whole year, others will extend for longer periods. These goals, selected by the general manager and his staff, are based on a critical analysis of the business's problems and the opportunities in the areas of cost reduction, product development, new manufacturing processes, new markets, product quality, organization, and staff. We provided this kind of structure so that the staff would look for balanced effort in all aspects of the business and would plan for it. The number of goals se-lected for the Large Jet Engine Department for this year is about 35 or 40.

The list of goals is made available to the next level of management. The staff takes the goals and repeats the process, adding whatever spe-cialized functional support needs to be accom-plished for the year. At the next level down we moved away from the word "goals" and said "work plans" instead. In carrying the process from the department general manager through the organization, we are attempting to decide: (1) what essential work this department must do to attain certain goals for the year; (2) what is the optimum organization, and how many people are needed, to make it happen; (3) what the manager must do to control the work while it is in process.

Throughout all of this, we've emphasized the importance of attaining a network of manager relationships. No manager can do his job in isolation. Almost anything that any one man-ager may elect to do impinges on his peers and his subordinates—and, many times—one or two levels up. So there is a constant emphasis on maintaining working relationships.

We've also talked a great deal with managers about their role as performance improvers. It isn't enough to hear what the subordinate is doing to follow his plans. The manager, in hearing it, must assess the adequacy of per-formance. He must assist the subordinate and, in nearly all instances, provide further inputs and redirect and recycle the work. At this point, managers must consider priorities of resources, schedules, and modifications of schedules. That is the kind of emphasis managers are asked to apply from the top down.

We have been working on parts of this process for about three years. This year represents the most thorough and complete implementation. It is now being applied throughout the man-agerial group, the exempt population; and this year we expect every office worker to have a work plan. The basic difference in our present practice is that the work plan or the goal for each individual within a department is linked to and identified with department goals. We get the linkage through all organizational levels. Also, from the top down, the department goals are made available to the next two levels; so there is an opportunity to constantly refer to and measure whether activities are geared to the things that the department general man-ager and his staff said were to be done this year.

Company Experience: 2. The B.F.Goodrich Company

Management by objectives has been a major technique at B.F.Goodrich for seven or eight years. J. W. Keener, president, per-sonally reviews and approves, or aids in re-vising, the objectives of the top 200 jobs. Clyde O. DeLong, who told this company case history at the AMA research workshop, was at the time assistant to the president and he had been manager of a Goodrich plant at an earlier point in his career. The account he gives of Goodrich's use of objectives in managing is, therefore, based on experience in both line and staff. He tells the story in these words:

Shortly after Mr. Keener became president, we restated what we call "The Policies and Objec-tives of B.F.Goodrich Company." We had, prior to that time, what were accepted as gen-eral policies and objectives, but we felt a need for definite statements in a form that could be published—basically, statements of our creed. I'm not talking about the objectives that are established for an individual in management *within* the company, but about the objectives for the *total* company. These involve many fields.

First, there are general objectives: what we expect the company to do immediately, and two years from now; five years from now; and looking further down the road. These are stated in growth terms: in volume of assets, in earnings per share, in improvement in earn-ings, in return on the assets that are assigned to the unit, and in the turnover in the dollars that we use. And there are statements of the policies under which these other objectives will be attained.

The next important area is marketing; that is, our policies and objectives as far as customers are concerned. These are statements of things that we will not tolerate and things we will, so that our people know what they can do. In the field of community relations, we state what we expect to do in the areas in which our plants are located; in the communities in which we operate; in our relations with local, state, Federal governments; and with the governments of the countries of our various international companies. We also issued clearcut statements of our policies and objectives so far as the buyer is concerned, and there were others.

So, you see, in developing policies and objectives for a total corporation you develop a document that will live for a great many years. Policies, if they're well thought out, don't change every time the wind shifts. I feel that, inasmuch as ours have stood the test of time over these six rapidly changing years, we have pretty good statements of company objectives.

B.F.Goodrich is not the largest rubber company in the world, but it is the fourth or fifth. We are primarily in the fields of rubber and plastics. Our operations are all over the world. We have associate companies in the international field, and we own many others outright or nearly so. We operate in about 26 cities within the United States. We have nine operating, profit-producing divisions, and we have other types of subsidiaries—a retail credit corporation, a realty company, and similar related interests. But, basically, our nine operating divisions are the business.

Now, to attain the objectives that are incorporated in this statement of policies and objectives, it stands to reason that at the divisional level these objectives have to be interpreted and stated in terms of specific things to be done. Our divisions are all manufacturing divisions. They have the responsibility for their own product development, their manufacturing, and their accounting, as well as their marketing. There is overall staff guidance from the corporate level in these activities, but basically all of our profit is produced by these divisions, except for dividends from minor investments in some of our foreign subsidiaries.

At this research workshop we are concerned with the application of objectives to the management level. At the top—the chief executive level—the objectives are stated on a long-term basis, not in dollars and cents but in the direction that we expect to go. We have a stated growth factor; market conditions in one year

may hold us back, but in the long pull we keep going in the right direction.

At the next level of management—the officer level—a vice president has a more clearly defined objective for the job he occupies. The lower the management level, the more specific the job becomes, and the fewer the job's responsibilities. It may even go down to where there's only one thing to do. That is, commonly, the clerical level.

Our formalized objectives involve approximately 200 top executives. How these objectives are to be attained we leave to the individual manager. A division head—who may have the title of either general manager or president of the division—has 10 to 12 specific objectives that are reviewed and approved personally by Mr. Keener. If the objectives need revision, through discussion with the individual Mr. Keener sees that they are revised.

To a query as to whether these are ongoing objectives, Mr. DeLong replied:

No, I'm talking about the objectives for one year. The ongoing objectives are for the chief executive level: the statements of policies and objectives published six or eight years ago. The objectives for the head of the division are stated annually for what we expect that division to do in that year, and the objectives must contribute to the profit and progress of the company. (Progress may be defined as "those things you do now that will result in profit or profit improvement in the future.") Specifically, these are things that have to be done now to attain the objective that may be five, ten, or even 25 years away. The head of the tire company has objectives set by the people who report to him, and they in turn by the people who report to them; so he will be able to attain the objectives that he has committed himself to attain during the year.

We started in 1958. By the end of the year we had defined objectives for about 200 people, stating what we expected them to do in 1959.

Frankly, I think we've been extremely successful in what we've done since then. We have just reviewed the objectives established and approved for the top 200 executives for this year, objectives that are direct and clearly stated. How far down this formalized objective program goes is determined by lower level management. Mr. Keener takes on a pretty good load in the responsibility for review and approval, redesign, and development of objectives for the top 200 jobs. You understand, the individual—the division head, say—first sets his own objectives; but in discussion with Mr. Keener these may be revised, and directly. Mr. Keener feels that the type of job definition that we are getting in these statements of objectives is vital to the real, down-to-earth, everyday management of the company.

We have found the program very successful. The first year we had a lot of hand-holding and wasted time. Our executives resisted: "Why pin us down? You hired us to do a job; now just hold up, go away, let us alone!" But, since their objectives would not necessarily be the objectives that Mr. Keener had for the assets that were assigned to them, the program and Mr. Keener's review continued.

"Organizationally, how far down does that top group of 200 take you?" Mr. DeLong was asked. He replied:

All the division heads are among the 200; then the second level—marketing heads, manufacturing heads, development, and so forth; and one or two levels below them. The plant manager of a large tire plant would be included, but not necessarily anyone below him. The 200 level would take in a few more executives in marketing. For instance, the tire marketing head would have a retail division under him, and the retail division manager would have about four regional managers across the country under him. But that's all the 200 would include at that level. I would say it would go a maximum of about six levels below the chief executive.

One listener in Mr. DeLong's audience inquired whether these organizational limits hold true for both staff and line.

Yes. I have been speaking about the operating man, the line man. For staff, I don't think we go below about four levels. I refer here to the corporate staff rather than the divisional staff.

Another member of the workshop session posed this question: "If the plant manager of one of your tire plants wanted to install a similar program for people who were reporting to him, could he do so?"

Yes, and they do; some a little better than others, as you would expect. Such an executive has committed himself to accomplish specific things. It stands to reason that in order to do these specific things, he assigns specific objectives to the various managers within that plant who report to him. It works very effectively.

Company Experience:
3. General Foods Corporation

At General Foods, job objectives are viewed as stimulators of added contributions to corporate goals. For attaining objectives beyond the standards set in their position descriptions, key people are rewarded through the firm's incentive compensation program.

Of particular interest in this company's approach are the "end results expected" statements which are incorporated in job descriptions and serve as standards of performance.

Review and evaluation by the manager are always done jointly with the individual. No set forms are used for this purpose, but guidelines are provided in a manual called "How to—for the Manager." Indicative of the nature of these guidelines is a section on standards of performance, in which it is suggested that the manager should:

Look for qualitative or quantitative terms of performance, such as:

Quantitative Terms
(Number, Percent, Amount)
· Factory door costs.
· Sales volume.
· New business.
· New products.
· Product complaints.

- New customers.
- Cost reductions.
- Production schedules.
- Turnover.
- Promotions.
- Market potential.
- Profit commitment.
- Safety record.
- Quality performance.
- Production efficiency.

Qualitative Terms
(Changes, Problem Solving, Ideas)

- Completeness.
- Requests for service.
- Complaints—praise.
- Cooperation received.
- Ideas generated.
- Changes initiated.
- Accuracy.
- Timing.
- Relationships established.
- Degree of acceptance.
- Problems and opportunities spotted.

Betty A. Duval, manager of personnel development, works with company managers to encourage increased effectiveness through the management by objectives program. Miss Duval tells the General Foods story for this report.

It is important to recognize that General Foods is a decentralized, marketing-oriented organization. The broad, company objectives are communicated to the divisions, with the understanding that each division develops its profit objectives, marketing plans, and budgets, which are then reviewed and revised in accordance with total corporate goals. When the division goals have been established, division management begins to work to achieve the objectives. It is hard to say whether objectives originate above or below, for corporate goals are influenced by management's knowledge of ongoing division plans and accomplishments. They really come from both directions—top-down and bottom-up. Some divisions may take several days to talk about their objectives and determine how each can contribute to their accomplishment. In the personnel division, for example, my boss has some objectives which he reports to the president. I have objectives which I establish within that framework. The

man who works with me has different objectives—again, in keeping with total department objectives. It should be pointed out that individuals are not limited to objectives stemming from the division or department objectives. It is hoped that they will use imagination and come up with contributions over and above their specific job responsibilities.

Very little has been *written* about objectives. In a letter written by an executive vice president to general managers some years ago, the guidelines were: "You are already committed to your profit plan and volume budget. This is your job. Now, over and above that, would you look for six to eight knotty problems or opportunities for improving the business, and establish these as your fiscal objectives. It could be longer than that—it might be a five-year plan—but indicate what portion you will get down this year." Thus an annual objective can be part of a long-range objective, provided it is so stated. Since this letter was written, more specific guidelines have been established for managers who want to use them.

We don't have forms for establishing and/or reporting objectives. Managers vary in their requirements regarding reports on progress. My vice president has changed the reporting period from quarterly to semiannual. However, he may talk frequently with us about our progress against objectives. We are free to organize progress reports as we wish, making them long or short. Other managers may require only an annual report.

Generally, the general managers and department heads ask key people in February to begin thinking about setting fiscal objectives for the beginning of our new fiscal year in April.

In accomplishing my own objectives, I may need the help of my assistant or others, and I may help him on his. However, the accountability for accomplishment rests with me or with him for our particular set of objectives.

We believe, too, that a manager can change his objectives, for a business can change. Suddenly, an opportunity that hasn't been anticipated opens up; so he may add an objective— or, on the other hand, he may eliminate one. This change is discussed first with his superior.

Individuals are encouraged to set deadlines

when they establish objectives, thus indicating when they think they will have accomplished a part or all of them. One object of deadlines is to help managers complete some of their objectives before the end of the fiscal year.

An interesting thing we found out through interviews with various managers is that the process of establishing objectives isn't too hard. It is in *planning* the accomplishment of the objective that managers have sometimes found the objective couldn't be accomplished as expected, or that it was going to cost too much money to get it done. So it is suggested that managers discuss *plans* for accomplishment ("Will the objective require manpower changes, additional equipment, additional expenditures, too much time, travel?") at the time they set objectives. As previously noted, our objectives need to be tied into our fiscal budget.

Now, about "payoff": the key position description outlines in broad terms what a manager is paid for in annual salary, and his salary increases are geared to his increased accomplishments and effectiveness in doing his job. The "end results expected" statements are what are sometimes called, in other companies, standards of performance.

In addition, a key person may receive at the end of the fiscal year a management incentive award which is based on his accomplishment of his basic position responsibilities and his *fiscal* objectives.

In working with managers, we are trying to focus on better planning for accomplishment of realistic objectives and more feedback and discussion of progress *throughout* the year. The idea of target setting (or goals or objectives) is established. We believe the real payoff is in increased involvement, commitment, and understanding by both superiors and subordinates in establishing and planning objectives and discussing progress.

In the "How to" section of its instructions for establishing objectives and evaluating results against them, General Foods outlines the responsibilities of both the manager and the individual who will work toward the objectives:

"How to"—for the Individual

Since "setting of objectives" is an established practice for key personnel throughout GF, most managers have communicated their own "preferred system" for having these established and reviewed, and having progress reported. Whatever system is suggested, the individual has the responsibility for considering and analyzing various alternatives in order to arrive at the most meaningful and realistic objectives.

Some suggestions made by key people which might be helpful to you in establishing objectives follow:

Review these specific sources for ideas:
- Position requirements, to avoid duplication and to highlight needs or points of focus beyond the routine scope of the job.
- Previous fiscal objectives, to avoid repetition.
- The department or division objectives, for possible ways to contribute.

Consider possibilities:
- Progress in the past year and areas needing further attention (unfinished projects and/or objectives).
- Problems and opportunities, within the function and your position, which need new solutions or approaches.
- Position requirements in a "state of development" needing special effort or emphasis.
- Prevailing circumstances which might influence objectives, such as: special market conditions, changing competitive activity and labor trends, changing technologies, the individual's experience.

Establish a tentative list of objectives and check each for its potential contribution to:
- Improvement of the business, or the function.
- Improvement of results in your position.
- Increased demands on you, making you learn, improve skills, and "stretch" yourself as a result.

Finalize for review with your manager:
- Decide on a selected few objectives which meet the above criteria, stating the general objective and what part of it is to be completed within the fiscal year.

- Check for uniqueness, that they are different from those submitted last year (unless special circumstances make continuing last year's important) and that they are in keeping with the job and the function.
- Set realistic target dates for each, indicating when, during the fiscal year, objectives will be completed. If an objective requires more than one year for accomplishment, subobjectives should be set for each fiscal year until completion.

Review objectives with your manager for approval, and revise as needed:

- Reach agreement with your manager on the desired format and the timing of progress reports and review.
- Notify your manager, at any time, of changes which require adjustment of objectives.
- Report accomplishment against objectives at specified periods.

Review your accomplishments against objectives at each period to plan your next period of work.

"How to" for the Manager

Whatever system is used for having objectives established, reviewed, and accomplished [the manager's], primary role is that of reviewing, suggesting, guiding, and questioning.

Some suggestions made by managers, which might be helpful, follow.

Necessary information: The general manager or department head may provide his key people with a copy of department or division objectives which is a framework from which the individual may get ideas for his objectives. The individual can make objectives which contribute to accomplishment of these division or department objectives, but he should not be limited to them.

Review objectives. You might raise some of these questions:

- How are the objectives different from last year's?
- Are they simply a restatement of a job responsibility?
- Will they contribute to the business?

- Will they bring something new to the job?
- Will they encourage the individual to think about something more than he has done before, and go beyond the routine scope of his job?
- Will these place extra demands on him as an individual?
- Will they require him to "work harder," "work smarter," or extend himself?
- Are they limited in number? Are they realistic and attainable within the period specified?

You can suggest the format in which you want objectives and accomplishments submitted.

Follow through.

- After the review, the individual modifies or revises his objectives, as required, before you submit them to the department or division head.
- The general manager or department head reviews all objectives to avoid conflict or duplication.
- You may supply copies of each individual's objectives to your staff members.
- Encourage the individual at any review period to adjust objectives as required.

SELECTED COMPANY STATEMENTS AND FORMS

Beginning on the following page are documents and forms used by six companies in developing and implementing their management by objectives programs. The six firms are Westinghouse Electric Corporation, New Holland Machine Company, The B.F. Goodrich Company, The Boeing Company, Yarway Corporation, and Calumet & Hecla, Inc.

OPINIONS ON THE WORTH
OF STANDARDS OF PERFORMANCE

Not every company that has installed performance standards and used them for a time has been satisfied with the results. Firms that have tried standards but subse-

(text continued on page 70)

WESTINGHOUSE ELECTRIC CORPORATION

Management Performance Objectives

[This is the policy and procedure statement issued by the company to guide its managers in setting up specific performance objectives (target plans) for all managerial ranks, from division manager or corporate headquarters department manager on down. Target plans for line management are developed before those of staff.]

GENERAL POLICY. It is the general policy of the company that management performance objectives are to be used in all organization units for all members of management. However, the specific procedures may vary from unit to unit. Because corporate and division objectives are on a calendar-year basis, target plans should also be on, but not limited to, a calendar-year basis.

APPLICATION IN A DIVISION

The first step in developing management performance objectives in a division is to establish the specific performance objectives, or target plan, for the division manager. After the objectives of a division have been approved for the year by corporate management, the group general manager and the division manager jointly establish a target plan for the year, toward which the division manager will direct his efforts. This target plan should be oriented toward solving the particular problems of the division and be directly related to criteria used for appraising the division's performance.

The second step is to establish a target plan for each individual reporting directly to the division manager. The procedure used is similar to that used in developing the target plan for the division manager. Working with each of his subordinates, the division manager jointly develops a target plan with each of them for the year. Each of these target plans should be related to the target plan of the division manager and thus to the overall objectives of the division.

A similar procedure is used for all other members of management in the organization unit. The target plan of each individual should be developed jointly with his immediate superior and should be related to the target plan of the superior.

It is desirable to establish the target plans for line management before developing those of staff management, so that target plans for staff managers can be designed to support those of the line managers.

After all the target plans have been established for the managers reporting directly to the division manager, he should review them as a group to be sure that they are compatible with each other and constitute an integrated, comprehensive plan for achieving the division's objectives. Similarly, the target plans for the subordinates reporting to a given manager should be reviewed by him as a group to be sure that they are compatible with each other and constitute an integrated plan for achieving the objectives of that unit.

It is recognized that much of the work in developing specific performance objectives at different levels of management can be done simultaneously.

APPLICATION IN A CORPORATE HEADQUARTERS DEPARTMENT. Management performance objectives in a corporate headquarters department should be accomplished in the same way as in a division. A target plan should be developed first for the manager of the department. His target plan should be related to the objectives of the company and to the objectives of specific units of the company which require the assistance of his department. Then the target plans for all other members of management in the department should be developed. All target plans within a particular department should be reviewed as a group so that they constitute an integrated plan for achieving the department's objectives.

GUIDELINES FOR ESTABLISHING TARGET PLANS

Individual target plans should be kept as simple and specific as possible. A relatively few specific performance objectives which can be kept clearly in mind are better than a long, complicated list of things to be done.

Achievement of the target plan by an individual should result in a distinct improvement in performance of the organization unit as a whole and of that part he manages. Therefore, the target plan for an individual should be related to the near-term and long-range objectives of the unit and of the company.

The specific performance objectives established for an individual should be those for which he can be held directly responsible. In some cases, however, it may be appropriate to establish the same specific objective for several managers who cannot be held responsible individually for its achievement. In such cases each manager should be told that he will be held responsible for achieving this objective both as an individual and as one of the group. This can be an effective means of promoting cooperation.

The specific performance objectives which comprise an individual target plan are of two types—quantitative and qualitative:

1. Quantitative objectives are those expressed in terms of "how much" and "when." There is usually more opportunity for the establishment of quantitative objectives for a line position than for a staff position, but quantitative objectives can be established for all positions.
2. Qualitative objectives are necessarily expressed in more general terms—frequently, "how well." These are not normally capable of precise measurement, but relate to the accomplishment of improvements which will favorably affect the company's near-term or long-range performance and profitability.

The key to achieving fairness in evaluating the performance of an individual is objectivity. A high degree of objectivity can be attained when an individual's performance objectives are expressed in definite terms so that data can be used to measure performance. Hence, most target-plan objectives should be quantitative.

Each target plan should be realistic, with the specific objectives representing realizable performance. At the same time it should reflect adequate improvement in the light of conditions and circumstances. A target plan which is so unrealistic that it cannot be achieved, or which provides inadequate improvement so that it can be achieved with little effort, is not fair to the individual, to others in the management group, or to the company.

Experience in the development and use of target plans indicates that the most effective plans are developed jointly by the individual and his immediate superior. Normally, the immediate superior should outline the general and specific objectives of the organization unit and his own target plan and then help the individual to develop his specific performance objectives within this framework. The individual's proposed performance objectives should be agreed to by both as the target plan for the individual.

ADMINISTRATION DURING THE YEAR

Each target plan is a management tool for the use of the individual and his superior. Both should have copies of the individual's target plan for ready reference.

During the course of the year conditions can change and thus affect the performance objectives in a target plan. When this happens, the target plan should be modified by the individual and his immediate superior. Compensating changes may also be required in the target plans for other individuals so that the achievement of all the target plans will still result in the achievement of the objectives of the organization unit. However, care must be exercised to avoid continually changing performance objectives, which may cause target plans to lose their significance.

Maximum benefits can be obtained by making the target plan the basis of regular performance reviews and by coaching and counseling throughout the year with the individual concerned. Such reviews yield two beneficial results: The manager can more effectively coordinate the efforts of the members of his management group, and the subordinate can obtain advice and guidance on his plans for achieving his specific performance objectives.

The target plan concept described in this guide is identical to the procedure used to carry out Step 1 of the annual performance appraisal program.

NEW HOLLAND MACHINE COMPANY

(Divison of Sperry Rand Corporation)

General Policy and Procedure: Management by Objectives

[A very detailed set of procedures for establishing, administering, and evaluating objectives in domestic and international units of the company. Reference is made to the desirability of setting monetary standards against which results will be measured. However, the emphasis in these instructions is on target dates and review —monthly, quarterly, and annually.]

Scope: All locations.

Purpose: To set forth the guidelines and the routine for establishing, administering, and evaluating objectives.

Introduction: Each division head is responsible for administering the management by objectives program within his division. The program involves submitting objectives at the beginning of each fiscal year, reporting progress during the year, and evaluating results at the end of the fiscal year. An effort should be made to include all key employees and all levels of supervision in the management by objectives program. Each division head will submit to the president and general manager his personal objectives as well as objectives from others which have sufficient importance to be included with total division objectives.

Definition: "Management by objectives" refers to a management method whereby management and supervisory personnel develop and establish goals for their operations at the beginning of each fiscal year. Management by objectives is not an addition to a manager's job; it is a means to improve performance of the job. Objectives do not normally include routine tasks for which a manager or supervisor is accountable. Instead, the objectives should be oriented toward goals of a creative nature, or special or "breakthrough" activities or innovations resulting from new technologies or new approaches to problems. Also, objectives may be oriented toward improved sales or profits, cost reduction, completion of specific projects, improvement in service, etc. In all instances it is desirable to establish a statistical or monetary value against which results can be measured.

RESPONSIBILITIES

I. Submitting Objectives

    A. Division heads

        1. Establish within division a management by objectives program in which designated key personnel and supervisors are to submit objectives at the beginning of each fiscal year.

        2. Request that objectives be submitted on the "Summary of Objectives" form in accordance with the following instructions:

            a. Prepare form in duplicate, and enter data required on form.

            b. Briefly and clearly set forth objectives *in sequence by target dates for completion.* (NOTE: Each objective must have a target date for completion. If date is beyond end of fiscal year, enter under target date the estimated percentage of completion at year-end.)

            c. List under each objective the key events and actions necessary to accomplish the desired result.

            d. Enter under "Statistical or Monetary Results Expected" a value, in dollars, which should result upon accomplishment of the objective.

        3. Submit objectives for the division to the president and general manager on the first day of the new fiscal year. Objectives should be in sequence by target dates for completion.

    B. Management personnel reporting to division head

        1. Inform all designated key personnel and supervisors to develop and submit objectives at the beginning of each fiscal year. (NOTE: To facilitate planning and internal control, individual objectives may be entered on the optional "Management by Objectives" form for submission and review.)

        2. Request each key employee to review and discuss objectives with the person to whom he reports and, when agreement is reached on objectives, to sign a copy of the "Summary of Objectives" or the optional "Management by Objectives" form.

        3. Review objectives submitted, plus others you develop, and select those to be submitted to the division head.

        4. Arrange objectives in sequence by target dates for completion on "Summary of Objectives" form, and submit to division head one week before the beginning of the new fiscal year.

        5. Discuss objectives with division head and revise as required. Obtain initials of division head on copy of "Summary of Objectives."

II. Review of Objectives

    A. Management personnel reporting to division heads

        1. Check monthly on objectives scheduled for completion the previous month. Follow specific objectives as required.

        2. Evaluate progress on all objectives quarterly, and report progress to division head.

        3. Prepare written evaluation of performance on all objectives at the end of the fiscal year. Submit report to division head one month after the end of the fiscal year.

    B. Division head

        1. Quarterly during the year, check progress on objectives for division.

        2. Prepare a report on the status of all objectives as of seven months after the beginning of the new fiscal year and forward report to president and general manager.

3. Review and evaluate performance on all objectives at the end of the fiscal year. Prepare a report on evaluation of performance and send to president and general manager six weeks after the end of the fiscal year.

THE B.F.GOODRICH COMPANY

The Position Objectives Program

[This guide sets the pattern for a statement of both quantitative and qualitative objectives. It suggests management areas that should be considered wherever applicable; reminds those who use these instructions that, although most objectives will be stated in terms of results during one year, long-range goals must not be overlooked; and stipulates a minimum number of objectives (six) for each manager.]

The program has two important functions:

1. It is a management technique for reaching a mutual understanding of each executive's responsibilities through the development and assignment of specific individual goals.
2. It establishes an objective basis for compensating executives according to their individual contributions to division and corporate results. Although there are several factors that determine the funds available for bonus distribution, an individual's achievement of his annual objectives is of major importance in deciding the amount of his bonus reward.

PROPER STATEMENT OF OBJECTIVES

Because of the major importance of the program, it is necessary that great care be given to the preparation of good objectives. The following guides are recommended:

1. At least six specific objectives should be established for each executive.
2. Those objectives are to include the individual actions and results most essential to achieving division and corporate goals.
3. The objectives should define reasonably attainable, but reaching, targets; that is, they must represent relatively optimistic goals, the accomplishment of which *will contribute significantly* to attainment of corporate and divisional objectives.
4. They should be stated in such a way that their performance can be clearly measured. This requires the use of precise and understandable terms, such as "Increase sale of X product line to 20% share of industry" or "Develop a fully qualified replacement for my own position."
5. The list should include both quantitative (How much?) and qualitative (How well?) objectives. Qualitative objectives are to be selected where applicable, *but at least several of each executive's position objectives should be qualitative.*
6. Although most objectives will be stated in terms of results to be achieved during the coming year, *it is important that long-range objectives not be overlooked.*
7. Specific target dates for each objective (or steps toward the objective) should be stated.

TYPES OF OBJECTIVES

An individual manager's list of objectives should represent a balanced management job. The following list includes examples of management areas that should be considered wherever applicable.

1. *Marketing objectives* (for example, sales, operating income, industry position, and expense targets).

2. *Production objectives* (for example, quality, productivity, and cost targets.)

3. *Financial and control objectives* (for example, inventory turnover ratios, credit and employment cost targets).

4. *Personnel objectives* (for example, organization, development, and motivation of personnel).

5. *Research, development, and technical objectives* (for example, product and process improvement; new product development projects).

THE PROCEDURE

1. Each eligible executive is to prepare a list of proposed objectives for his position and submit it through customary channels to his division head.

2. The immediate supervisor is to review the proposed objectives in a meeting with the executive and agree on a final listing. The division head will submit two signed copies of this form to the director, organization development.

3. The lists of objectives will be reviewed by the president, the executive vice president, and the appropriate group vice president. If it is felt that a list needs further study or clarification, it will be returned to the division head for that purpose.

4. The immediate supervisor will retain copies of the objectives in his files and will review them at least twice during the year in interviews with the individual executives. Interviews should be carefully planned in advance to cover all the listed objectives, should emphasize the compensation opportunities of our "reward and penalty" principle of incentive compensation, and should include a discussion of the steps to be taken to reach those objectives not currently on schedule.

5. If circumstances require a revision of an individual's objectives during any year, such revision should be made, and the director, organization development, should be notified of the change.

6. At the end of each year, a date will be established for the submission of final evaluations of performance along with bonus recommendations.

7. The use of this "Position Objectives" form for positions not included within the Executive Incentive Compensation Group is encouraged. Its use offers important advantages in addition to administration of compensation.

THE BOEING COMPANY

Aerospace Group, Electronic Operations

Procedure for Implementing Objectives for One Year

[The steps to be followed by the management of the division in developing and implementing yearly objectives and the form used in recording and following up are included here.]

ACTION STEPS REQUIRED TO CARRY OUT THE OBJECTIVES FOR 19____

1. Each organization head is asked to share with the electronics operations manager the full responsibility for accomplishing the overall objectives for the year.

2. Each organization will develop its own goals and programs for supporting and implementing these objectives. This should be done by February 15.

3. Each manager or supervisor will make certain that the people working with him know the goals of his organization and the resources, performance standards, and time available to accomplish them.

4. Each member of management will define his own job primarily as doing what he can to help achieve the overall objectives of electronics operations and the corresponding objectives of his own organization.

5. As a step in defining his job he will develop, with his superior, specific objectives for his assignment. This should be done by March 1. Many of these objectives will be identical to, and all will be compatible with, those of his organization.

6. Each manager and supervisor should check each activity against this criterion: does this particular use of our resources (time, money, material, personnel, facilities) contribute meaningfully to our aims for the year. If it does not meet this criterion the action should be seriously questioned and perhaps cut out.

7. Each member of management is responsible for controlling his work to the established standards. When he becomes aware that we will miss a target he should make corrective action on this problem a main order of personal business. He can do this by carrying out his own delegated work properly in the problem area; by preparing action suggestions to others in a position to correct the problem; by offering his personal help to the organization involved.

8. Periodic appraisal of managerial performance will be made, using as a yardstick the extent of contribution made to objective.

9. One outcome of the appraisal will be a personal development plan for each person which will increase his ability to contribute to the accomplishment of objectives.

10. Management forums will be held to discuss methods and problems in managing this total program.

11. Periodic progress reports will be issued to each manager or supervisor showing how well we are accomplishing the overall objectives. These reports will be rough estimates drawn from our normal control systems. A more precise report is unnecessary since its purpose is to inform each member of management if we are moving in the right direction and on the right timetable.

12. Revision will be made to match changing conditions. Special attention will be given to the need for revision at the time of the periodic progress report.

13. Each organization is expected to merge its efforts with other organizations in accomplishing these objectives. Total end-results as defined in this document, rather than functional excellence, will be the measure of our work this year.

YARDSTICKS FOR INDIVIDUAL OBJECTIVES
    (Requested in Item 5 Above)

1. The objectives point to the results of effort, not activities. They describe goals rather than pathways.

2. They are within the range of your responsibility and authority. It is appropriate for you to take the actions required to attain them.

3. They can be used to measure how well you are performing, at least to the point where you can distinguish failure from success.

4. They tie in and contribute to the objectives of your organization and of electronics operations.

5. They are fair, realistic, and attainable.

6. However, they also require effort and skill to reach them, and extraordinary effort on your part to surpass them.

7. They are part of an improvement curve that takes you beyond your previous attainment.

8. They call for the proper balance and mixing of work, compelling you both to meet today's spread of commitments and to build a strong organization for five years from now.

9. There are not too many objectives. Your choices are limited to the vital few which will make the most difference in your operations.

YARWAY CORPORATION

Planning Guide

[The company's description of the planning process used in developing a first formal statement of objectives.]

INTRODUCTION

This planning guide has been developed as a means of giving direction and purpose to the work of all members of the Yarway organization.

1. It is intended to establish a set of objectives for the entire Yarway organization.

2. It is intended to promote unity of effort by helping all Yarway people to recognize their mutuality of interest and interdependence in achieving the established objectives.

3. It is intended to provide a continuing measure of performance for use as a yardstick of success in achieving the established objectives.

4. It is intended to serve as a "living document" subject to wise improvement and revision to meet changed circumstances and new opportunities as they arise.

The sequence of events leading to the development of the planning guide can be described briefly as follows: On November 1, 1962, the board of directors elected D. Robert Yarnall, Jr., president of Yarway Corporation. In February 1963 he appointed a management committee representing each of the major line and staff functions of the company. Recognizing that planning is one of the first responsibilities of management, the management committee embarked on a study of the company's strengths and weaknesses and future needs and opportunities as a basis for forward planning.

The management committee worked diligently from February through September, meeting one or two days each week, and the planning guide was developed as a tangible and potentially useful result of these joint efforts. An initial draft was prepared for presentation to all members of Yarway management—the group of approximately 100 people with supervisory and/or professional responsibilities—at a meeting on September 28, 1963. In the month following this meeting a high proportion of the management group responded to the invitation to submit their reactions, comments, or questions on the planning guide. After careful study of these thoughtful responses the management committee worked out a final draft which reflects the thinking of all members of Yarway management. This draft was approved by the board of directors on December 4, 1963.

Perhaps it would be well to record the management committee's procedure in developing this document. As a focal point for initial discussion, the committee first posed the following basic question: "What should the company we are building be like ten years from now?" This question was subdivided into a number of manageable pieces, and the committee developed an outline for the project that helped us to "put first things first."

Following our outline we first reviewed the *Statement of Basic Policies for Yarway Corporation* adopted by the board of directors in December 1959 and revised in June 1961. From this starting point we proceeded to think through very carefully the responsibilities of management with respect to our customers, employees, stockholders, suppliers, and community. This was followed by an equally careful and far-reaching effort to spell out clearly and specifically the objectives of the company. After much discussion we agreed upon objectives in terms of sales volume, profitability, market standing, products, and capability and productiveness.

Our next step was to make an intensive study of the resources of Yarway Corporation. We identified our resources as follows:

1. Yarway people (knowledge, skill, attitudes, and growth potential).
2. Yarway product lines (competitive strength and growth potential).
3. Trends in our present markets.
4. Reputation or image of the company (in present and potential markets and in the labor market for employees).
5. Know-how (technical, marketing, and manufacturing).
6. Patents.
7. Agreements and contracts.
8. Physical assets.
9. Financial assets.
10. Nature of stock ownership and control.

We, the members of the management committee, studied each of these areas in depth in an effort to arrive at a fair and objective assessment of our strengths and weaknesses as a company.

Then, while keeping our objectives and our resources clearly in mind, we worked out what we have called *Development Guidelines for Products and Markets*. The development guidelines for products spell out our collective judgment as to the industries we should concentrate on serving, the customer needs we should concentrate on satisfying, and the criteria we should use in selecting new products. Under the section on development guidelines for markets, we have included the policy on government business which we worked out earlier this year.

We fully recognize that planning is only one step in the attainment of the objectives we have set for ourselves as a company. A well-coordinated program of planning, no matter how carefully developed and clearly understood, does not in itself assure success in reaching established objectives. Therefore, the final step in this project was to identify and clarify the major growth activities which we must perform simultaneously and successfully if we are to achieve our company objectives. Because these major growth activities are companywide in nature, we have taken special care in assigning responsibility to the appropriate member of the management committee for coordinating each of them.

We cannot afford to forget that our future success as a company will have to be earned, the same as the successes the company has enjoyed in the past. Our ability to develop a new success pattern of our own in the years immediately ahead will clearly depend upon the capability and will to achieve that we possess both individually and collectively.

With this in mind we have been anxious to have as much participation as possible by Yarway people in determining the direction we should take to achieve future success, so that all members of the organization will share a common purpose and a firm resolve. We want what we do in the future to be born of the belief that it is what we should be doing.

OBJECTIVES OF THE COMPANY

Sales Volume: Total volume of Yarway products sold throughout the world (not including production of licensees) should increase at an average rate of 7% per year. This will result in just about doubling sales volume in ten years.

Profitability: Net profit should average at least 7% of sales (shipments) and 11% of net worth.

Market Standing

The company should achieve and maintain as large a share of the market for each product line as can be done at those prices which will permit the company to realize its profitability objectives. The company should become the highly regarded primary supplier as soon as possible after release of the product for full-scale marketing.

The company should not become dependent on any single customer for more than 10% of its sales volume or on any single industry for more than 20% of its sales volume.

Products

New products are those which conform to the product development guidelines of the company. They should be released for full-scale marketing at an average rate of at least one per year.

Product-line improvements, extensions, additions, or eliminations should be made as required to achieve and maintain the market standing and profitability objectives of the company, or to take advantage of unusual opportunities to utilize more productively the company's resources. In performing these activities the product development guidelines should be approached to the extent that it is practical to do so.

Capability and Productiveness

New and better capabilities—both individual and organizational—should be developed each year in marketing, manufacturing, engineering, administrative, and management activities. (This refers to our ability to do *new* things.)

Greater output for a given input of human, physical, financial, and information resources should be achieved each year by each segment of the company. (This refers to our performance record in doing the things we have been doing.)

CALUMET & HECLA, INC.

Division A

Objectives (One Year)

[These statements show how the objectives of the company functions are derived from the overall objectives for the division, and how responsibility for the accomplishment of certain objectives is held by more than one function.]

Earnings before taxes: $X

Gross assets employed: $Y

Rate of return on gross assets employed: $\frac{X}{Y}\%$

Capital expenditures Class I allocation: $Z

OPERATING OBJECTIVES

1. Number of customer complaints on commercial business should not be more than X% of orders billed. Dollars of settlement should not exceed Y% of total commercial billings.
2. Review of management controls reporting system by July 1.
3. Period costs not to exceed $X per week.
4. Program to maximize and expand standard gross margin dollars in product lines A, B, and C.
5. Obsolete items and all adjustments to inventory not to exceed X% of commercial sales dollars.
6. Five specific examples of improvement in cost or salability of nondefense products.
7. Sales of nondefense items: X minimum. Sales of defense items: Y minimum.

AREAS OF SPECIAL CONCENTRATION

1. Develop new products program by October 1, working with corporate vice president, marketing and planning, and corporate vice president, research and engineering.
2. Materials control function effectively operating by June 1, working with corporate vice president, administration; corporate vice president, marketing and planning; and corporate vice president, manufacturing.
3. Program to simplify order processing techniques by October 1, working with corporate vice president, marketing and planning; corporate vice president, manufacturing; and corporate vice president, administration.

Finance Objectives (One Year)

1. Direct and coordinate functions to surpass Division A's minimum objectives of:
   Net profit: $X
   Net sales—nondefense: $Y
   Net sales—defense: $Z
   Net sales—total: $Y + $Z
2. Operate within established and approved annual budgets.
3. Establish new quality control program as fundamental part of finance's thinking and action.
4. Participate with all divisions to increase average standard P/V ratio for all products from X% in preceding year to Y% in current year.
5. Provide more useful and better services and control data through improvement in current programs and through an advanced, but completely practical and economical, redefinition and re-establishment of the systems function.
6. Establish a systems department with responsibility for complete programing of new EDP applications. Staffing to be completed by March 1.
7. Re-evaluate the further capability to mechanize the processing of business data compilation and frequency of feedback reporting presently being done on a manual basis (program target date: April 1):
   a. Accounting and cost reporting for maintenance work orders.

b. Accounting and cost reporting for tool requisitions.

c. Accounting and cost reporting for all appropriation requests.

d. Inclusion in mechanized backlog the added capability to produce standard gross margin by element of product line, by acknowledged shipping date to customer and detailed listings of delinquencies in meeting acknowledged shipping dates to customers.

e. Mechanical preparation of gross margin contribution in new order receipts, backlog, gross shipments, customer returns and allowances, and reported net sales.

f. Mechanical accumulation of marketing and sales functional costs for mechanical preparation of reports comparing order intake, customer returns and allowances, and reported net sales versus functional marketing expense incurred by sales territory and/or by product manager.

g. Mechanical processing and daily reporting of active classified inventory receipts, disbursements, reorder quantities, stock-outs, etc., by part number (in order to eliminate the need for manual processing of data and bookkeeping on the materials control Wheeldex records).

8. To improve variance reporting system to include (program target date: June 1):

a. Analysis of total volume variances to account for effect of sales product mix, sales price variance.

b. Analysis of total cost variances to account for effect of materials purchased price; materials usage; labor efficiency; spoiled work; utilization by substitution of slow-moving, classified inventory items.

c. Effect of small volume orders on work standard efficiencies, using improvement curve theory techniques.

d. Effect of increased costs created by lack of lot control in processing shop orders.

e. Analysis of material scrap reporting on basis of yield resulting from input-output reported data.

9. Program, schedule, and publish updated property ledgers as recently redesigned. Program target date: February 15.

10. Develop a more meaningful system of order coding to maximize the capability and output of the data processing equipment. Target date: February 15.

11. Continue the refinement of forecasting and profit-planning techniques with the objective of an integrated flexible budget program.

12. Study and evaluate the various elements used in the preparation and consolidation of forecast and profit planning data to determine the capability for mechanization of such data where practicable. Program target date: April 1.

13. Develop and publish a budgeting manual, including flow charts and procedures, to more clearly define the basic data required of the various elements of the Division A organization, the formats in which the data are prepared and submitted, the approvals required, and the deadline dates to be observed for data presentation. Target date: August 1.

14. Refine the development and application of "improvement curve theory" data to the development of more competitive cost/price factors. Program target date: February 1.

15. Restrict bad debt losses to less than X% of reported nondefense sales.

16. Target the average age of accounts receivable not to exceed 35 days; limit the past due portion of total trade accounts receivable to 20%; maintain minimum rate of eight turns of accounts receivable per annual rate of sales.

17. Conduct and complete a study throughout all functional divisions to identify and evaluate all unused and/or surplus wooden office furniture and equipment; and complete a study to

determine the investment cost to replace all presently "necessary and assigned" wooden furniture with a standardized complement of steel furniture. Program target date: July 1.

18. Reduce finance division induced returned material by effectively contributing to Division A's goal of
   a. Reduction in number of customer complaints from an average of X per month in preceding year to Y per month in current year.
   b. Reduction in dollar value of credits for returned material from an average of $X per month in preceding year to $Y per month in current year.
   c. Reduction in dollar value of cost of returned material credits from an average of $X per month in preceding year to $Y per month in current year.

19. Improve finance's skills through participation by finance management in outside seminars, workshops, and plant visits (one meeting per year per individual).

Engineering and Development Objectives (One Year)

[Note that the first four objectives are the same as those of the finance and manufacturing divisions.]

1. Direct and coordinate functions to surpass Division A's minimum objectives of:

   Net profit: $X.
   Net sales—nondefense: $Y.
   Net sales—defense: $Z.
   Net sales—total: $Y + $Z.

2. Operate within established and approved annual budgets.

3. Establish new quality control program as a fundamental part of engineering and development's thinking and action.

4. Participate with all divisions to increase average standard P/V ratio for all products from X% in preceding year to Y% in current year.

5. Establish a product development department solely devoted to new product and product improvement development. Staffing to be completed by July 1.

6. Select, with the president and general manager and the director of marketing, one wholly new product and initiate development. New product to be on the market in three years or less.

7. Select, with the president and general manager and the director of marketing, at least five specific product improvements and release them for production during the current year.

8. Establish, with the directors of marketing, manufacturing, and finance, product value improvement teams with specific objectives for improving salability of all product lines. Program target date: January 1.

9. Complete evaluation of the Division A patents and applications and review quarterly with the president and general manager and the director of marketing. The first review, by February.

10. Rearrange the laboratory to effect a more orderly work environment and management control. Program target date: March 26.

11. Reduce E&D division-induced returned material by effectively contributing to the Division A goal of:
   a. Reduction in number of customer complaints from an average of X per month in preceding year to Y per month in current year.

    b. Reduction in dollar value of credits for returned material from an average of $X per month in preceding year to $Y per month in current year.

    c. Reduction in dollar value of cost of returned material credits from an average of $X per month in preceding year to $Y per month in current year.

12. Reduce E&D Division overtime premiums incurrence from $X in preceding year to $Y in current year.

13. Improve engineering skills through participation by E&D management in outside seminars and workshops (one meeting per year per individual).

Manufacturing Objectives (One Year)

1. Direct and coordinate functions to surpass Division A's minimum objectives of:
Net profit: $X.
Net sales—nondefense: $Y.
Net sales—defense: $Z.
Net sales—total: $Y + $Z.

2. Operate within established and approved annual budgets.

3. Establish new quality control program as a fundamental part of manufacturing thinking and action.

4. Participate with all divisions to increase average standard P/V ratio for all products from X% in preceding year to Y% in current year.

5. Achieve further substantial improvement in manufacturing quality, delivery, and costs.

6. Develop manufacturing engineering into a dynamic technical organization. Program target date: July 1.

7. Improve planning, scheduling, and dispatching through installation of more effective procedures and through formalized training of personnel.

8. Reduce order delinquency rates to the point where they do not exceed the following in the current year.
Product line A: X%.
Product line B: Y%.
Product line C: Z%.
Product line D: X%.

9. Install lot control plan by January 1, and have it functioning effectively by July 1. Labor performance to be at standard based on improvement curves by July 1.

10. Reduce purchase costs from previous year's experience as follows:
    a. Production hardware: X% minimum.
    b. Supplies: Y% minimum.

11. Reduce inventories X% in current year as related to inventory levels reported on December 31 of previous year. This achievement to be exclusive of major programs specially approved or discontinued during the year.

12. Establish with the directors of marketing, engineering and development, and finance, product-value improvement teams with specific objectives for improving salability of all product lines. Program target date: January 1.

13. Reduce manufacturing division overtime premium incurrence from $X in previous year to $Y in current year.

14. Reduce manufacturing division induced returned material by effectively contributing to the division goal of:

    a. Reduction in number of customer complaints from an average of X per month in previous year to Y per month in current year.

    b. Reduction in dollar value of credits for returned material from an average of $X per month in previous year to $Y per month in current year.

    c. Reduction in dollar value of cost of returned material credits from an average of $X per month in previous year to $Y per month in current year.

15. Install and make operational the automation program in product line A. Program target dates: Phase I, January 15; Phase II, May 1.

16. Install and make operational the production line for assembly of products in product line B. Program target date: January 1.

17. Eliminate redraw and related operations on product line B. Program target date: May 15.

18. Conduct comprehensive study of all product line B manufacturing and make recommendations for improvement. Program target date: April 1.

19. Improve manufacturing skills through participation by manufacturing management in outside seminars, workshops, and plant visits (one meeting per year per individual).

(text continued from page 55)

quently decided to abandon the practice give several reasons. Some top executives—William Bynum, president of Carrier Corporation, for one—find standards "too theoretical." Bynum stated that, in his opinion, "the basic question is whether managers get the job done or whether they don't." In another large firm, the manager in charge of management development reported: "We tried using standards, but without much success. We stopped for many reasons, but perhaps the most important was that we judged that the cost of the effort was far in excess of the value we were deriving."

Lester F. Zerfoss, director of management services at American Enka Corporation, attributed his company's discontinuance of formalized performance standards to a change in its management philosophy:

Under the former management, which was headquartered in New York, we were interested in formalizing procedures; that is, we had job descriptions and performance standards in some departments. At that time this approach seemed to have some value. With a new president and new management, viewpoints have changed. The new president is sales- and customer-oriented. Our company has been moving so rapidly, it would have been impossible to maintain the paperwork needed to keep changing standards of performance up to date. Now our approach to setting standards is more flexible. The company depends more heavily on the personal communication between the supervisor and his employees to determine standards. Personal contacts have increased. This approach increases motivation; makes people stretch, makes them use more of their abilities.

Despite occasionally heard reservations, explicit and agreed-to standards of performance are being used more and more. Each time an objective is set for a major responsibility, a new standard has been set; each time an earlier objective is allowed to continue without change, a standard is continued. And, for jobs which have been without established standards, the first attempt to set them represents a major commitment to what are, in effect, objectives.

How Companies Proceed
In Setting Standards

The classic approach to setting standards of performance is to:

1. Call together the people on the job for which standards are to be set.
2. Identify, with those concerned, the major responsibilities of the job and the tasks to be performed in meeting each responsibility.
3. Identify and select measurements which will indicate the level of performance on each task.
4. Set the measurement values which will represent standard performance.
5. Establish procedures for collecting and reporting to job incumbents the measurements which will indicate their levels of performance.
6. Organize so that job incumbents have the authority to take remedial action if needed in order to meet their standards of performance.

The pattern of action in setting up standards of performance has been reported for this research study by seven companies: three manufacturers, two utilities, an airline, and a life insurance company. Statements and forms used in drawing up standards will be found at the end of this chapter.

Otter Tail Power Company

This case history related by Albert V. Hartl, president of Otter Tail Power Company, indicates how fully a program of standards of performance has been integrated with his firm's planning, budgeting, and personnel procedures. Hartl also implies that launching such a program is likely to encounter some employee resistance at first, since the advantages of standards of performance are not all obvious; acceptance takes time. He says:

It should be emphasized that this process tends to be a joint supervisor-supervised project. Initially, this undertaking has involved preparation of job descriptions as a prerequisite to establishing performance standards. We are confident that the use of job descriptions, performance standards, and objectives gives employees more complete knowledge of their work, provides a better understanding of how well they are expected to perform, and enables them to accomplish more because of the objectives which they themselves helped develop.

Currently, Otter Tail Power Company is completing standards for most first-line supervisory jobs. This includes written standards for district managers and plant superintendents. . . . Performance standards for officers and major department heads are not yet finalized. . . .

Otter Tail Power Company first investigated the performance-standard technique as long ago as 1954. Since then, development of performance standards and objectives has been a slow but continuing process which has received more and more acceptance as company personnel have come to recognize its advantages and benefits.

Marathon Electric Manufacturing Corporation

R. V. Jones, president of Marathon Electric, is another who gives strong support to the use of standards of performance. For his company, too, the use of standards is closely integrated with other management procedures. Jones describes Marathon Electric's approach as follows:

During the past three years—after my first management briefing session—we started to prepare job descriptions and standards of performance. The president and other top corporate personnel attended the four-week AMA Management Course, and during this time we prepared our job descriptions and standards of performance. Our "second line" (junior management) has since attended the Management Course. We now have job descriptions and standards of performance for all salaried employees.

These, of course, are a long way from being perfect, but with continued work we expect them to be of considerable usefulness in the next two or three years.

Detailing the procedures he has used at the officer level, Jones said:

First, in the preparation of the job descriptions and standards of performance, each executive reporting to me set down what he thought his job was. This was reviewed with me and changes were made and approved. The job then was reviewed with the top management team, which consisted of the president, vice president of marketing, vice president of finance, vice president of engineering, vice president of manufacturing, and the manager of purchasing (now director of materials). We all became educated in each other's jobs.

We expect to accomplish, through job descriptions and standards of performance, appreciation for each other's jobs. . . . If each of us accomplishes our standards of performance, we shall be better managers and our company will earn better than average return on investment.

As in all human endeavor, there have been problems too:

The greatest difficulty is to get at the job. I don't think there are too many people who like to put down a set of standards that they are going to be judged by each month or each year. However, once one becomes accustomed to this method, he finds it is very advantageous to himself as well as to the company. I know it was very difficult for me to sit down and write standards for myself, and I think that has been true for each of our salaried employees. . . . Even today, I do not think the standards have been developed to the degree that they should be, but we have made a start in the direction of better management. . . . The standards must be constantly reviewed, and with a yearly appraisal they should be improved and be of more value, *provided those employees involved do it.*

. . . as of this time, I can say the results are beneficial to both the employee and the company; the employee does a better job, since he now knows what his boss and company want.

In most cases, he has received an increase in salary. Better paid, he naturally does a better job for the company, and the end result is a more profitable company—which is, of course, the management job.

American Airlines

The use of standards of performance is not restricted to any one type of organization. Approaches vary, however, to fit an organization's requirements. This fact is highlighted by American Airlines. Peter M. Herman, manager, methods and standards, described extensively his company's approach at the research workshop held as part of this AMA study:

As you know, American Airlines handles both passengers and air freight. In addition, we have a wholly owned subsidiary which specializes in airline catering.

We have about 25,000 people and are presently doing about $590 million of business; about $530 million in passenger revenues and the balance in air freight, mail, and express. We are, basically, a decentralized company. However, we do have a centralized staff which includes our finance and planning department. It is the central staff which sets our general objectives, decides what kind of performance we want to give our customers, and determines policy and procedures.

Our decentralized group is made up of the various cities that we serve. We operate out of 35 cities—in the case of New York City, out of three airports. Each of these cities is headed by a city manager who has full responsibility for that operation. In Ford Motor Company or General Electric, a decentralized division is responsible for producing a certain return on investment. We cannot do that. We do not say to Los Angeles that we want a 10 percent return on investment in that station. This is because many of the expenses that are generated in Los Angeles may affect other parts of the country. Since one of our major expenses is aircraft which operate through several stations, it would be almost impossible to allocate the expenses of these aircraft to any particular station. This is true of many of our other expenses. This reason—among others—has made us very dependent on the use of performance standards to measure the city manager's performance.

Let's go back up to the top of the organization again and discuss objectives: The chairman of the board—our chief executive officer—sets up certain long-range (five-year) objectives and policies. These are generally the share of the market and return on investment, such as 10.5 percent or whatever the CAB will allow us. Below these objectives are subobjectives to help in their attainment. One of the most important is the level of customer service; in our company, in our industry, it's the lifeblood. There are still other objectives, such as the number of aircraft we intend to make available over the years.

Reporting to the chief executive officer are two groups; the operating department, headed by the corporation president, and the finance and planning group, headed by our executive vice president of finance. This organization serves several purposes, and it works very well. The operating group in turn is composed of two organizations: marketing and operations. The operations group manages aircraft maintenance, and the pilots and similar personnel. The following discussion will be limited to a consideration of the performance standards used by the marketing group, for it is the marketing organization that is responsible for the performance of our city managers.

Let us return to the major objectives which were set by the president in the five-year plan: they are translated by our two major vice presidents (marketing and operations) into more detailed objectives which are then turned over to each of their operating people (the department heads).

The department heads will outline what they propose to do to accomplish these goals—a program for that year and programs for each of the next five years, which are incorporated into a long-range plan. Programs may encompass the kind of stewardess services we will provide; the kind of reservations policy we will maintain; and so on. Through these programs we get our innovation. Each department head can develop any program he wants to and be as creative as he wants to be, within the limits of the overall company policy which has been outlined by the chairman of the board.

After these plans have been set up—the operating plans for the year—they go back to the department heads and up to the president.

Now, on our performance standards activities: When we talk about performance, we like to break it up into two closely integrated areas—one, of course, is *cost performance* standards, and the other is *quality* standards. As stated before, our main objectives are to earn a certain return on investment and to pay a certain dividend. And, to get the best sales results, we have to offer certain kinds of product quality to our customers. This is where we introduce our quality standards. For example, we feel that to get the best business in reservations away from our competitors, it is necessary that 90 percent of our phone calls be answered within 20 seconds. This standard is based on the judgment—most of it intuitive—of our top management. In all our functional areas, whether baggage loading or greeting people at the airport, or selling tickets at the ticket office, we have certain quality standards. These are dynamic in that they can change from year to year, depending on the competitive situation. (I don't say that, if the competitive situation deteriorates, we're going to reduce this quality level.) The higher the quality level, obviously, the higher the cost. Our line management is responsible for maintaining these quality levels, which are the basis for the managers' performance appraisals.

My department, methods and standards, gets involved when the head of a functional group—our director of reservations, for instance—decides that the company should maintain a certain level of quality in his area. We will then cost it out, and accordingly he will decide whether the company can afford the price tag, basing his decision on several factors—competition, for example. Then, if this quality level is accepted by management, we will set up cost criteria which state that for this kind of standard, line management will have to spend this much money. Assuming certain inputs in reservations—such as the number of phone calls he expects to get—the line manager will know how much he can spend to achieve the quality level. Thus we have a cost performance measure;

he's allowed to spend this much money to maintain this quality level.

We like to think that over a period of time our standards are such that, to maintain this quality, the manager is not going to be able to spend less. When he is able to spend less, we reward him for it. We look at our standards and adjust downward or upward so that, over a long period of time, the chances are that this manager will spend no less and no more to maintain a certain level of service.

We stress not only manpower; we get involved in all expenses, whether for material, equipment, or other items. In most cases we have as a basis of performance a tie-in between cost and quality. In other words, a manager can make quality at a certain cost level. The way this works is that, at the beginning of the year, operating plans are sent out to the field. These indicate the number of aircraft which will serve a given city, the number of passengers they can expect to board, and the like. The field puts together a budget based on the appropriate cost and quality standards. Their objective will then be to achieve this quality standard for this workload and at this cost level. The budget comes back to the staff for review. If we, as staff, can make improvements, we'll suggest them. When the budget is approved, it becomes the operating plan for the year. Then, of course, we go through month by month and compare the plan with the actual, both cost and quality. The performance reports first go to the city manager where they are reviewed with his subordinates. The supervisors try to find out why they didn't make standard, so that they can improve their performance. The monthly reports are forwarded through the city managers to the group vice presidents and up to the president. From these reports the president knows the general company performance, both quality-wise and cost-wise; he will go back to management and take the necessary corrective action to insure that future performance is up to desired standards.

I would say that 80 percent of the manager's appraisal is based on whether he makes these two integrated standards, cost and quality.

Right now, most of our quality standards are systemwide; in other words, all stations have the same. We hope some day to become sophis-ticated enough to adjust this situation. Perhaps we will find that the tolerance of our customers in one station is different from that in other stations, and that therefore we may have different levels of service among the stations.

Asked how long American Airlines has used this approach, Mr. Herman replied that at least certain aspects of its program dated back eight or nine years. Another question followed: "Has performance improved as a result of the program?" The answer was:

Take reservations, for instance. We have several levels or measures of performance. First of all, in comparison with our competitors we've done fairly well in both profit and quality; so in that aspect of the job our performance has improved. However, we like to think of our quality performance as staying fairly level. In other words, if our object is to answer 90 percent of the calls to a reservation office in 20 seconds, we will accept that standard with no further improvement. We try to improve our quality only when our competition changes performance levels. Then we may raise or lower ours.

"But if the standard is not met," said the questioner, " 'personnel action' follows?"

Mr. Herman replied, "Yes. If performance standards are not met, there usually is some kind of management change."

One member of the workshop stated that he had gained from this discussion an impression that the airline sets the standards for its people without their participation, and asked Mr. Herman if this were true and if so, if the managers had no part in a possible adjustment of the standards. Mr. Herman responded: "Because our staff personnel have a total perspective of the company operation, they are charged with the responsibility for setting standards. However, field personnel generally will provide local feedback, which is then used by staff to re-evaluate present performance objectives."

Another question followed: "An interesting point, however, is that the impetus for setting an objective comes from your marketing people when they tell you what quality and service requirements are necessary to be competitive. They can subsequently suggest changes in requirements?"

In answer, Mr. Herman reminded his audience that cost and quality overall objectives of American Airlines are set by corporate management, but other goals come from market managers in given cities and are developed with general headquarters. Although there are differing markets, the same quality standards obtain throughout the system.

The point was pressed. "Do you see any opportunity really, for the individual to pass made norms? It seems so cut and dried. You set these overall, systemwide standards, and if the managers meet them they can keep their jobs. Is there any opportunity for them really to pass the standard? Do you provide motivation for the manager to pass the standard?" The reply:

Let me give you an example—again, in reservations. Certain standards are cost-oriented. We spend a set amount of money to maintain this standard, and we will do no better and no worse; it is designed that way. If the managers perform better than standard over the long run, something is wrong. However, there are other quality standards; in reservations there

are five or six standards which are not cost-oriented. For example, the quality of the conversation and attitude of the agent toward the customer can vary greatly. We may say that, 90 percent of the time, our people should talk to the customer in a certain way to achieve standard. But if a man does better than standard, it doesn't cost us any more or less. If a station does not meet this performance or is doing better, that's where a man can improve performance yet hold the line on costs. Of course, people will be recognized for this kind of performance.

Asked how to measure quality of conversation, Mr. Herman answered:

This is based strictly on the subjective opinion of our supervisors in conjunction with certain guidelines provided by staff. In addition, we have a performance rating team, made up of general office staff personnel from various functional groups, which goes from station to station to insure uniformity of quality. We know we have uniformity of quality by the fact that a manager made 90 percent of his calls in 20 seconds; that's a measurable, tangible standard. But, to make sure that we do have a uniform standard of performance in the intangible areas such as customer conversation, we have a performance rating team going around from office to office. Telephone calls are monitored periodically.

Forms used by American Airlines in measuring performance and reporting it against standards are reproduced on the following pages.

AMERICAN AIRLINES

The Performance Measurement and Reporting Program

PURPOSE AND SCOPE

In a large, complex company like American Airlines each manager cannot constantly observe all the activities for which he is responsible. To overcome this handicap, we have set up a program to measure both quality and spending performance against *established standards* and to report the level of performance to our managers.

These reports tell staff managers how well they have planned our policies and procedures; they also tell line managers how well they have carried out these policies and procedures. The quality of the service we are providing and the cost of that service are clearly revealed. When needed, changes in policies and procedures can be made or corrective line action can be taken.

PERFORMANCE MEASURES AND REPORTS

Performance is measured and reported in three areas—quality, spending, and volume—as described in the following paragraphs:

1. *Quality performance.* There are two types of quality performance measures:
   a. Those that measure activities with a direct impact on our customers (for example, baggage delivery).
   b. Those that measure activities without a direct impact on our customers (for example, load computation).

   The quality performance measures and their standards are established by the general office (see "Responsibilities" below).

   Each month the performance of each city is measured against the standard for each quality measure applicable to that city. Each resulting performance measure is normally expressed as a percentage which can be equal to, greater than, or less than the standard. This performance is reported each month to line management at the city and to the general office, where it is published in a report entitled "City Performance Report—Quality."

   Some quality measures may cover activities that are the responsibility of more than one manager. In these cases the objective is to measure the total performance resulting from the combined effort of all managers involved.

2. *Spending performance.* Each month the actual expenses of a city are compared with the planned expenses (budget) in the following three spending reports:
   a. Spending performance detail—location/branch/line.
   b. Spending performance detail—city/line.
   c. City performance report—spending.

   These three spending reports are sent to the cities as well as to certain general office personnel.

3. *Volume.* Included on the "City Performance Report—Spending" are statistics on passengers boarded, departures, air freight pounds loaded. The actual figures for the month are shown along with the forecast figures; thus, managers can know how the actual workload varied from the expected workload in these three areas.

To aid in the analysis of each city's performance, each city also submits monthly comments explaining the major deviations from standard in its quality and spending performance.

RESPONSIBILITIES

1. *Establishing performance measures and standards.* The director of management information is responsible for developing and designing *all* quality and cost performance reporting systems for all levels of management, including necessary forms and procedures. The following functional authorities in conjunction with the director of management information in New York City are responsible for determining what quality measures will be made:

Activity	*Functional Authority*
Reservations Ticket offices Ticket lift and ramp Load and clearance Baggage delivery and mishandling	Director, ground passenger services
Cabin service Food and catering services	Director, in-flight service
Aircraft maintenance	Assistant vice president, line maintenance
Aircraft cleaning	Director, maintenance operations center, TULE
Automotive and ground equipment	Director, engineering services, TULE
Line cargo Cargo services	Director, cargo service

Quality measures and standards will be established or changed only after evaluation using the planning procedure.

No change will be made in the quality performance measure workload at any city without the approval of the director of management information in New York City, and the appropriate functional authority listed above.

2. *Local variations in quality standards.* Local variations in system quality standards for your city may be authorized by the functional authorities listed above. If you have justifiable reasons for not being able to achieve the system quality standard, proceed as follows:

   a. Make studies to assure that the failure to make standard is not the result of poor methods or of poor use of personnel and equipment.

   b. Find out the highest level of performance you can attain with your present manpower and equipment and the cost of manpower, equipment, or both needed to attain system standard.

   c. Send a letter to the functional authority concerned requesting a local variance in the quality standard. Include with the letter all the above information and copies of the studies made. Send a copy of *all* this material to the director of management information in New York City, and send a copy of the request letter to the vice president, sales and the service/regional vice president in New York City.

AMERICAN AIRLINES

Airport Ticket Office (ATO) Quality Performance

STANDARDS

1. *Waiting time:* At least ____% of customers arriving at an ATO ticket counter shall be waited on within ____ minutes.

2. *Baggage mishandlings:* Baggage mishandlings by ATO ticket salesmen, sky caps, and ticket lift agents shall not exceed one per _____ checked and rechecked bags.

3. *Customer impact:* At least ____% of ATO customer contacts shall be rated acceptable.

4. *Posted flight arrival times:* At least ____% of the flight arrival times posted in the "Will Arrive" column on the arrival board shall be accurate to the degree that the actual arrivals will be within ____ minutes before or ____ minutes after the time posted.

5. *Posted flight departure times:* At least ____% of the flight departure times posted in the "Will Depart" column on the departure board shall be accurate to the degree that the flights will depart prior to or within ____ minutes after the time posted.

6. *Ground transportation availability*
    a. When limousines are scheduled by flight, at least ____% of all limousines shall have enough seats for customers and will depart within eight minutes from the time the last bag was placed on the claim counter.
    b. When limousines are scheduled on a headway or regular schedule, at least ____% of these limousines will have enough seats for customers and will depart on schedule or within the established headway time.
    c. When taxis are the only form of ground transportation, at least ____% of all incoming flights will have enough taxis available so that all customers will be accommodated within ____minutes from the time the last bag was placed on the claim counter.

American Brake Shoe Company

In January 1965, American Brake Shoe Company had about 25 percent of its executive group covered by standards of performance, yet a standards program has existed in this firm for six years. Such slow acceptance of a program which is in the process of being "sold" seems to be a general finding. But no one suggests that other than a selling approach be adopted.

Joseph T. Gresh, assistant director, management personnel, reported for this research study the company's method of setting standards of performance. It is an example of what may be called the classical approach. It is straightforward:

1. *State job functions and responsibilities.* The man on the job and his boss prepare separately, but with the guidance of a personnel staff executive, a list of the major responsibilities of the job. In doing this they have started at the top of the organization unit in each case and have worked down.

2. *Select measurements.* After reaching agreement on the major responsibilities, the same individuals agree on the measurements which will be used to de-scribe performance. These are as specific as feasible. For a sales position, for example, they would include share of market, profit goals, management of controllable expenses, and other similar matters. When necessary, procedures are established to collect data which are needed for measurements but are not available.

3. *Establish performance standards.* Again, the group involved agree on the measurement value which will represent standard performance.

4. *Compare results with standards.* Once the decision is made as to what measurements will be used, thereafter routine control reports indicate actual results and planned results or standards. The variances uncovered in this comparison lead to action: either performance is improved or, on a quarterly basis, standards are revised.

Gresh has developed techniques that he has found effective in selling—not imposing—American Brake Shoe's approach. In one application of his method he asks operating people: "What would you like to know, or to measure, if this was your own business?" The attitude implicit in this question pleases operating people. He also emphasizes, whenever possible, that the measurement program is aimed at the problems of "running the job," not at personality characteristics. This, too, is an attitude that operating people accept.

Gresh thus summarizes the major value of the company's program: "It helps move us from the subjective to the objective." The objective approach, he feels, is essential to a sound management effort.

The Cleveland Electric Illuminating Company

The Cleveland Electric Illuminating Company first used standards of performance in 1947. Since that time it has revised and improved its procedures and has applied them to additional units of the company and to more levels of management.

This company's program derives from the basic theory that measurement is fundamental to control; that control requires a knowledge of the objective (the reference point for control); and that the standard of performance is the measurement value which indicates whether results are contributing to the achievement of the objective.

S. E. Wertheim has summarized the program in a memorandum to group, division, and department heads of the firm. The following excerpts are relevant.

1. Measures and standards of performance are management tools used to control the implementation of plans and the achievement of objectives. They are signals which indicate when management must analyze the situation and take corrective action to improve performance.
2. The establishment of standards requires the participation of at least two levels in the organization. The supervisor and the subordinate must mutually understand the objectives to be attained and the system of measurement and standards which will be used to judge performance. In significant plans it is important that not only the plan and the objective be written

down, but also the system of measures and standards. Time should be spent now, for example, reviewing the objectives and systems of measures and standards in the budget planning reports.
3. The system of measures and standards for a particular objective should be complete and should surround the area being controlled. A system of measurement and standards should cover quantity, costs, unit costs, and quality. The measurement system may be numerical, but in many cases it may have to be a verbal statement of the conditions which exist when performance is considered to be well done.
4. Some objectives and systems of measurement and standards are independent of the level in the organization. More often, a statement of an objective and the system of measurement and standards at one level must be translated and modified to be significant at the next lower or higher level in the organization. As an example, rate of return is a significant measure at the corporate level but is not a significant measure at the vice presidential and lower levels.
5. The period covered by the measurement system must be appropriate to the period of the activity being measured. There are some company activities where accomplishment is measurable many times a day. The system should be appropriate to these differences, in spite of the fact that we are all required to report on a monthly basis in performance analysis.
6. Measures and standards should be related to the most important things being undertaken in any area of activity. It would be helpful for each manager to list the five most important things which he expects to accomplish and to ask: How do I know whether these things are well done?
7. One of the most useful controls, from a management point of view, is the control of time and how time is used. A system of measurement in this area would tell what activities are being accomplished and how long they take. Standards in the area can be engineered, historical, estimated, or market.
8. Standards should be reviewed and revised when work methods, or the activity, sig-

nificantly change. The cost of the system of control should be consistent with the value of the activity being controlled.

9. Very often, it is more economical to record data about an activity on a continuing basis, even though the time period for control purposes is much less frequent. The frequency with which the measured data are compared with standard and used as a control may vary, depending on how good the performance is.(9)

Rockwell Manufacturing Company

Rockwell Manufacturing Company has had a well-organized program of standards of performance since 1962. R. F. Dean, director, organization planning, describes the company's approach:

Performance standards have been established for all managerial positions, from the president down. These are reviewed annually. All of our managers have been involved in this program since its inception. It is their responsibility to prepare, or have prepared, a form entitled "Position Description and Performance Standards" for all the people (managers) reporting to them. Normally, this is prepared by a manager (for his own position), who must then meet with his supervisor to secure his approval regarding the responsibilities, weights of these responsibilities, authority, and the standards which are established. There must be agreement between these men regarding responsibilities, standards, etc. Our purpose is to improve the performance of managerial personnel, and our experience has been that the techniques we are using have done this.

In the process of setting up and using standards, this company has encountered problems similar to those faced by many other firms. Says Dean: "Our main problem has been to get managers, and the people who report to them, to establish realistic objectives and attainable standards for all positions. We feel that we are making prog-ress in this area but there is more work to be done."

He adds, however, that one of the major advantages of such programs has been achieved: "The requirement to establish objectives and standards has required managers to look more critically at the positions for which they are responsible and to take positive action to meet both their short- and long-range objectives."

An instruction sheet used by Rockwell in preparing position descriptions (weighting each responsibility, assigning authority classification, and preparing statements of performance standards) is reproduced here.

Connecticut General Life Insurance Company

Henry Dawes, director of personnel for Connecticut General, describes this company's use of standards of performance as "a way of life." He adds: "A man is more likely to reach his destination if he knows where he is going."

In the approach used by Connecticut General, objectives, strategy, quotas, results, measures, and standards of performance are all aspects of one management process: *plan, and work the plan.*

Standards of performance were first used by this firm in 1958, starting with jobs at the middle management level. They were quantitative wherever it was possible to make them so; nevertheless, most of the initial standards were qualitative. (Qualitative standards proved to be easier to prepare in realistic terms and therefore enabled the program to develop more rapidly.)

With increased managerial sophistication, however, standards have become increasingly quantitative. They are divided into standards of performance relating to long-term goals (which most companies would call objectives) and those relating to short-term goals and the projects involved in accomplishing them.

Dawes reports a favorable attitude on the part of supervisors: He says they "enjoy sitting down to discuss standards with their subordinates. It's the best technique for delegating, we've found. In discussing performance, no finger is pointed at anyone. It's common for the employee to bring up the suggestions on how he will get better results."

Guidelines for developing performance standards at Connecticut General Life Insurance Company are reproduced here.

Forms and statements used by five other companies in developing standards or reporting their results make up the balance of this chapter. In length and abundance of detail they range from a brief and simple form for reporting an appraisal, to a very explicit set of standards for measuring the separate segments of—for example—a secretary-treasurer's responsibilities. As in other instances, some of the complete forms originally provided by the companies were overlong for the scope of this report. Accordingly, in such cases only enough of the form to show the general plan of procedure is reproduced here.

CONNECTICUT GENERAL LIFE INSURANCE COMPANY

Extracts from Standard Practices and Procedures: Performance Standards

In most cases, supervisor and subordinate should work together in setting the job's standard. One of the greatest values of such joint action is a mutual understanding of goals. When the subordinate does the initial writing of the standard, he gains a refinement and clarification of the objectives and priorities of his job. He may be more willing to accept the standard as fair if he takes an active part in drafting it. Under some circumstances it may be preferable to have the supervisor prepare the first draft.

The ultimate responsibility for the standard, however, lies with the supervisor. He sees the broad scope of overall objectives for the area and has a better understanding of priorities. He also has sufficient experience to counteract the subordinate's tendency to set too high a standard.

In cases where several individuals occupy similar jobs it may be best for all of them to participate in the writing of the job standard, at least as far as the common elements are concerned. The manager should be in on this from the beginning, however, lest the group become fixed in a wrong idea of what the job's standard is. Another way of writing the standard for such similar jobs is to assign the most articulate member of the group to the task of synthesizing the ideas of all into a standard.

In some instances, as with a new job or a new employee, it will have to be pretty much the supervisor alone who writes the standard.

How to Go About Writing the Standard

Getting started is generally a problem in writing a job standard. One solution is to start with a brief statement of the job's basic objective. For example: "To plan and direct the sales program in order to achieve the highest possible profitable sales volume at the minimum practical selling cost." Another suggestion is to start from the job description, which serves as a checklist for the tasks on which you will set the standard. The pitfall in this approach is the difficulty of breaking away from the descriptive language of the job description.

In any case, the job should be broken down into its major subdivisions or tasks and then standards should be set for the activities involved under each.

Having listed the subdivisions or tasks, the next step is to put into writing a clearcut, simple statement of the conditions that would exist or the results that would have been achieved if performance had been satisfactory. For example:

Task	Standard
Establishment of controls	Periodic reports are established and submitted by the tenth of each month; they give an accurate picture of operations and indicate trends.

In developing standards we are trying to answer the questions: How well? How many? How soon? In what manner? Are we stressing results on a job and attempting to develop measurable standards?

Quantitative and Qualitative Standards

It is difficult in many cases to set a standard that is measurable for every task. Research on past results sometimes eases the task. For example: "The sales manager's job will have been satisfactorily performed when his territory obtains 10% of the market."

Objective: Recruit men for management training program.

Standard: Placement officers are cultivated, and an interest in Connecticut General is created among the students, to the end that
1. An average of eight seniors seek interviews at each campus.
2. Cancellations of scheduled campus interviews amount to less than 10%.
3. 10% of those seen on campuses are offered jobs.

When Results Are Not Measurable

In certain instances, the end result of a job is not directly measurable. For instance, the results of a training program may not be subject to measurement. However, the job should be carried out in a certain way if it is to give results. It is better to measure a man against methods than against a set of personality traits. For example, the standard, "Letterwriting course results in a 20% improvement," cannot be measured; the standard, "Participants in letterwriting course express enthusiasm and three months after conclusion cite improvements in their practice," can be measured.

Yearly Objectives

Some standards will stand up year after year. On many jobs, however, projects are undertaken from time to time and a standard can and should be established for each such project. For example:

Task	Standard
To prepare a manual of performance standards.	This job will have been satisfactorily performed when: A manual is issued which is clearly written and which assists the various supervisors and employees in preparing useful standards. Success in meeting this standard will be measured by the use to which the manual is put.

Points to Keep in Mind

1. Prepare standards for only the principal functions of the job.
2. Standards should be attainable by the average incumbent. A standard should be something that can be exceeded by superior performance. Perfection is not standard.

3. Where possible define such words as "effective," "satisfactorily," "liberal share," "efficient."

4. Job standards are not easy to write, and your first effort will probably not satisfy you. Constant refinement and experience will be necessary before the standard is satisfactory.

Having built up a rational case for standards, it might be unwise to conclude by suggesting that you should not belabor the writing of standards. The tendency will be to attempt to be extremely specific and all inclusive, yet very simple general statements of standards are effective in obtaining improved performance and are effective management tools. The important thing is to get away from ratings by personality traits and to concentrate on the results expected of the job. Don't expect to be able to write standards that will take away from the superior his job of using judgment; all you can do is channel that judgment.

THE WESTERN COMPANY

Standard Practice Instructions: Position Guide

POSITION TITLE: Secretary-treasurer and manager-finance.

ACCOUNTABLE TO: President.

BROAD FUNCTION

The secretary-treasurer and manager—finance is accountable to the president for successful and efficient conduct of all finance and accounting functions and for the required financing of the company. He is reponsible for providing advice and counsel on company financial matters. He is responsible for the successful and profitable conduct of data service operations.

Is responsible to the president, board of directors, stockholders, and courts for detecting, notifying, and following up to see that proper action is taken so as to prevent fraud, embezzlement, misappropriation of funds, and the like.

Within company policies he is responsible for and has commensurate authority and accountability for:

1. Development and recommendation of financial policies.
2. Performing all financial functions of the company, including accounting, budget compilation, internal auditing, reporting, banking, safekeeping, office services, cash receipts and disbursements, credit and collections, accounting methods and statistics, financing, insurance, and payrolls.
3. Serving as secretary for the company.
4. Serving as treasurer for the company.

PRINCIPAL RESPONSIBILITIES

A. *Secretary*
   1. Maintain minutes books of corporation and issue certified copies of resolutions as appropriate.
   2. Attend board of directors' meetings and stockholders' meetings, and record minutes of the proceedings.
   3. Sign and attest certificates, statements, and reports.

4. Issue notices of board of directors' and stockholders' meetings.

5. Make arrangements for meetings of the board of directors and stockholders.

6. Liaison with attorneys.

7. Liaison with statutory state agents.

8. Maintain stockholders list.

9. Accept service of process.

B. *Treasurer*

1. Banking relations: Recommend depositories for company funds. Maintain cooperative relations with personnel of banks and other financial institutions.

Measures for Accountability	*Standard*
a. Quality of recommendation.	*a.* Approved.
b. Number of complaints.	*b.* Number.
c. Confidence in treasurer.	*c.* Line of credit and interest rates.

2. Capital expenditures: Approve release of funds when available for capital expenditures.

Measure for Accountability	*Standard*
Action taken.	Yes or no.

3. Cash flow: Formulate disbursement procedures for accounts payable, payrolls, and the like.

Measure for Accountability	*Standard*
Take maximum discounts with lowest bank balance while maintaining satisfactory credit with suppliers.	Percent of discounts taken.

4. Contracts: Review contracts for financial, tax, and risk considerations when requested.

Measure for Accountability	*Standard*
Problems as result of inadequate review.	Number.

5. Custody

   a. Act as custodian of funds of the company.

Measure for Accountability	*Standard*
Valuables secure.	Approved system for security and losses.

   b. Act as custodian of securities, notes, mortgages, patents, contracts, insurance policies, or other such documents.

Measure for Accountability	*Standard*
Important contract documents centrally located and secure.	Approved system for security and losses.

   c. Establish surety bond requirements.

Measure for Accountability	*Standard*
Action taken.	Losses.

6. Investment: Recommend the most advantageous use, including timing, of the company's cash resources.

Measure for Accountability	*Standard*
Percent of cash invested.	Return on investment.

7. Financial control

   a. Recommend action to maintain equity position and working ratios in the long-term best interests of the company.

Measure for Accountability	*Standard*
Written recommendation.	Approved.

   b. Plan future cash and financing requirements.

Measure for Accountability	*Standard*
Written recommendation.	Approved.

8. Financing

   a. Arrange for needed short-term borrowing.

Measure for Accountability	*Standard*
Action taken.	Terms.

   b. Arrange long-term loans.

Measure for Accountability	*Standard*
Action taken.	Approved.

   c. Formulate and negotiate details of capital financing transactions.

Measure for Accountability	*Standard*
Action taken.	Terms.

9. Insurance: Determine and administer insurance program covering all assets and risks.

Measure for Accountability	*Standard*
Completeness and cost of coverage; program in balance.	*a.* Approved by president.
	b. Number of uninsured losses compared with saved premium.
	c. Loss ratio of those items and appraisal of the risk and service cost.
	d. Ratio of uninsured losses to cost to insure.

10. Real estate

   a. Purchase, sell, and lease property as instructed.

Measure for Accountability	*Standard*
Action taken.	Yes or no.

   b. Negotiate, approve, and pay real estate and personal property taxes and assessments.

Measure for Accountability	*Standard*
Action taken.	Yes or no.

11. Signature

   a. Sign checks.

Measure for Accountability	*Standard*
Action taken.	Yes or no.

   b. Sign and cosign contracts, stock certificates, and other such documents.

Measure for Accountability	*Standard*
Action taken.	Yes or no.

12. Taxes

    a. Detect effect of tax changes on the company's operations.

        Measure for Accountability   *Standard*

        Promptness of detection of changes.   No added cost through lack of anticipating effect.

    b. Keep responsible positions informed and take appropriate action to minimize taxes.

        Measures for Accountability   *Standard*

        1. Action taken.   1. Yes or no.

        2. Minimum taxes.   2. Dollars.

    c. Develop and recommend most advantageous use, including timing, of changes in laws and regulations.

        Measure for Accountability   *Standard*

        When minimum taxes are paid.   Tax trends.

UNIVIS, INC.

Vice President for Distribution

[Univis lists detailed performance standards for its vice president of distribution concerning inventory management, service, delivery, production, financial results, policy, organization management and administration, and special assignments. The standards for production performance and financial results are listed here.]

PRODUCTION PERFORMANCE

Satisfactory production performance will be attained with respect to receiving, handling, and delivering of the company's products and the furnishing of reports when this division has established and maintained a trend in the improvement of its handling, storing, and delivering techniques and the utilization of the computer, operating at a level consistent with expected sales levels and utilizing equipment and manpower to a high degree. Relative importance to job: ____%.

1. A product handling installation, capable of handling a maximum of _____ units per year, will have been developed and available by December 1 of the current year. This includes space, equipment, and the nucleus of personnel for the installation.

2. An order processing installation, capable of handling a maximum of _____ orders per year, will have been developed and in operation by December 1 of the current year. This includes space, equipment, and the nucleus of personnel for the installation.

3. Normal production requirements are achieved in a normal work week with the equipment available to the division.

4. Handling, storing, delivery, and the production and furnishing of reports are maintained at a normal and even flow when the volume of work handled on any two days of a normal work week is not more or less than ____% of the normal requirement of the week and when the work volume on the other days of the week is not more or less than ____% of the average for the week.

5. Operational standards have been established for ____% of the hourly paid employees and selected weekly paid employees.

6. Production standards are established for the volume of work to be performed on daily, weekly, and monthly bases.

FINANCIAL RESULTS

Satisfactory financial performance will be attained when the product orders and reports are handled at a unit cost of less than that experienced in the previous year; when utilization of total assets including inventories are not in excess of ____% of the standard amount allowed for the operation of this division; and when continued progress is indicated toward reduction of costs of operation and increased utilization of assets. Relative importance to job: ____%.

1. Consolidated value of finished goods inventory during eight months of the year does not exceed the value of such inventories at December 31 of the previous year. The value of inventories in four months of the year does not exceed by more than ____% the value of finished goods inventories at the end of December 31 of the previous year. The average inventory for the current year does not exceed by more than ____% the value of inventory at December 31 of the current year.

2. The capital assets used by this division do not exceed the total of such assets as of December 31 of the previous year.

3. The space requirements (square feet) of this division do not exceed the space utilized as of December 31 of the previous year.

4. Established financial policies of the company are adhered to.

5. Division costs are held within budget levels and there is an indicated trend of cost reduction.

6. The average cost of processing an order, including shipment of material, does not exceed $_____ for frame orders and $_____ for lens orders.

7. The average cost per unit shipped, including orders processed and handling, does not exceed $_____ for frames (fronts) and $_____ for lenses.

8. A study is made to determine the cost of handling frame products and has resulted in the decrease of such costs.

TRANSCON LINES

Standards of Performance for the President

[Transcon Lines sets up very detailed standards of performance for its president. They cover financial results and resources, policy development and administration, planning, investment, organization and management development, resources, and communication. The sections dealing with his responsibilities in handling financial results and resources, in planning, and in organization and management development are reproduced here.]

FINANCIAL RESULTS AND RESOURCES

A. Satisfactory performance has been attained with respect to return on net worth when

1. The company maintains a rate of return equal to or exceeding its stated policy.

2. The company maintains a rate of return which, when measured by a ten-year moving average, is a continuing upward trend.

3. The profit margin of the company is better than the average of the top 25% of its principal competitors as tabulated in its yearly comparative review.

B. Satisfactory performance has been attained with respect to financial strength when

1. Working capital is adequate, but not excessive, as measured monthly by the maintenance of a ratio of current assets to current liabilities of at least 1.5 to 1 (this minimum to be acceptable only during a reasonable period following the assumption of obligations during a substantial expansion); at any time such current ratio shall have exceeded 2.2 to 1, the president will submit to the chairman an adequate and detailed plan for the investment of excessive funds in conformity to the long-range investment plans promulgated by the chairman.

2. All debt maturities coming due within a 12-month period are adequately covered by the financial plans representing the use of internally generated funds, or specific plans for meeting such obligations have been presented to the chairman.

3. Cash and its equivalent are maintained at a level not less than equal to current liabilities.

4. Funds to cover estimated expenses for taxes and licenses are accrued monthly and reserved in a separate bank account and held as unusable for other purposes.

5. Total debt (including unsecured notes due within one year and equipment obligations due within one year) does not exceed one and one-half times the net worth.

6. Charge-off for depreciation expense exceeds by 15% or more the payments made toward equipment obligations.

7. Excess funds not reasonably necessary to the day-to-day operation of the business, as indicated by forecast cash needs, are placed each month in the corporate account and reserved in that account for withdrawal only upon the authorization of the chairman.

C. Satisfactory performance has been attained with respect to financial availability when

1. Bank credit available from principal depository banks is at least twice the amount of the bank debt outstanding. (This does not imply that such bank credit shall be supported by a definitive bank credit agreement, but it may be supported by lines of credit or other indications of availability.)

2. There are available to us sufficient and satisfactory sources for the financing and purchase of terminal facilities to be leased back from the purchaser and owner to satisfactorily meet our needs for improvement or expansion.

PLANNING

A. Satisfactory performance has been attained in relation to planning when

1. The president presents to the chairman at least annually prior to the beginning of each year a definitive operation and financial plan for the forthcoming year.

2. These plans include
   a. Sales goals: (1) sales plan and (2) advertising and sales promotion budget.
   b. Profit objectives.
   c. Operating expense budgets.
   d. Major operational expansions.
   e. Major proposed investments for equipment or facilities.
   f. Specific objectives that cover the company as a whole as well as each of its principal segments.
   g. Courses of action for attaining objectives.

    h. Availability or attainability of resources and other elements required for attaining objectives.

    i. Major personnel or organizational changes or developments.

3. These plans are

    a. In writing.

    b. Approved by the chairman and/or board of directors prior to the beginning of each calendar year.

    c. Reviewed periodically in the presence of the chairman and/or board of directors.

ORGANIZATION AND MANAGEMENT DEVELOPMENT

A. Satisfactory performance has been attained in relation to organization and management development when

1. Functions required to run the business have been divided into positions which are described and coordinated in properly approved organization charts, position descriptions, and management guides which are kept currently up to date.

    a. A periodic review ascertains that the approved basic plan of organization, authorities, and responsibilities is observed and carried out.

2. Authority is delegated to the positions where decisions can be most competently made so that day-to-day operating problems do not require the president's immediate attention.

3. Each executive who reports to the president has standards of performance which have been approved by the president.

4. The management positions required to run the business are filled by individuals competent to run it to the satisfaction of the chairman without the president's having to spend time doing the work of weak performers.

    a. The chairman has been provided with opportunities to become acquainted with officers, potential officers, and other key executives and to evaluate the abilities of those men.

    b. Recommendations for officers are accepted by the chairman.

    c. There is an identified supply of qualified and trained replacements.

        (1) There is a formal, organized, and actively administered management development program, which includes appraisal of individual potential.

        (2) There is evidence that a candidate whose qualifications for promotion or transfer have been established prior to the time a vacancy occurs has been identified for each managerial position now covered by the executive bonus program. (For this purpose one person may be a candidate for more than one job.)

        (3) There are enough qualified men available for management and advisory positions to assure that company growth in accordance with long-range plans is not deterred by any present or potential shortage or inadequacy.

5. The president provides an environment that inspires the highest possible group and individual manager performance through

    a. A regular program of periodic review of performance with individual managers, coupled with corrective action where it is found to be necessary.

    b. Executive incentive and compensation plans.

    c. Working relationships.

    d. Personal example.

ROCKWELL MANUFACTURING COMPANY

Position Description and Performance Standards: Instruction Sheet

TITLE: (Of position)　　　　　　　DATE:
NAME:　　　　　　　　　　　　　SECTION:
PREPARED BY: (Signatures of incumbent and supervisor)
DEPARTMENT:
APPROVED BY: (Signatures of incumbent and supervisor)

MAJOR SEGMENTS OF POSITION (*What individual has to do*)	WT. %	CLASS 1 2 3	STANDARDS OF PERFORMANCE (*Conditions that will exist when each segment is performed satisfactorily*)

List here major segments of position in the order of their importance. Opposite each segment, in the column headed "Wt.," show the weight it bears to the whole job, such as 5%, 10%, 15%, 20%, etc., of the job. The weights for all segments should total 100%.

After showing the weight for a segment check in one of the columns under "Class" the authority normally exercised in carrying out each segment according to the following classes:

Class 1. Complete authority. Actions to be taken without consulting supervisor.

Class 2. Limited authority. Supervisor must be informed of any action taken.

Class 3. No authority. Supervisor must be consulted before action is taken.

Following is an example of how one segment of a personnel manager's position could be reported.

1. Develops and administers wage and salary programs.

In this column list opposite each segment what conditions will exist when the segment has been completed satisfactorily. These standards should be in achievable, measurable accomplishments, such as those supported by production schedules, quotas, quality, quantity, expense, time, records, etc.

When writing standards of performance, the emphasis should be placed upon the *end results*—of each segment, rather than upon the steps which are taken to carry out the segment. There are a few situations in which it is not possible to set standards in terms of actual results to be attained—for example, some segments of a research engineer's job. In such situations standards may be set as to what a man should do to accomplish the segment. The assumption is that, if he goes about his work in the right way, everything will be done that can be done.

1. Performance is satisfactory when

a. Area surveys have been conducted at specific time each year.

b. Wage and salary structures are developed and approved.

c. Programs are administered in accordance with approved procedures.

(WT. % = 30; CLASS = X)

WHIRLPOOL CORPORATION
Plant Manager's Standards of Performance

JOB RESPONSIBILITY	STANDARD	PERFORMANCE			WORK PLANS AND REMARKS
		FIRST QUARTER	SECOND QUARTER	FIRST SIX MONTHS	
1. Maintain efficiency in the work force to a level of	97%	97.2%	98%	97.6%	Continue developing the full-day work concept with the hourly employees.
2. Operate to a quality index level of	70	82	89	85	Work on process #1 for continued improvement.
3. Control perishable tools per man-hour worked so it does not exceed	18¢ per man-hour	18¢	17.5¢	17.75¢	Work with tool engineers for continued tool life improvement.
4. Control scrap percentage of the direct labor dollars earned so it does not exceed	.095%	.08%	.07%	.075%	Continue present program.
5. Control factory supplies per man-hour worked so it does not exceed	9¢ per man-hour	8.5¢	8¢	8.25¢	Continue present program.
6. Maintain variables as budgeted:					Second six months' goal: $74,025. Continue scheduling programs to achieve new goal.
First quarter	$43,153	$45,477			
Second quarter	$35,820		$28,480		
First six months	$78,973			$73,957	
7. Control unscheduled overtime so as not to exceed	$84.00 per week	$87.50	$86.50	$87.00	Establish more frequent scheduling meetings.
8. Control lost hours so as not to exceed	$325.00	$245.00	$105.00	$175.00	Plan to average better than goal.
9. Maintain safety standards to the extent of no lost-time accidents and a reasonable amount of medicals		11 medicals, no lost time	10 medicals, no lost time	21 medicals, no lost time	Continue emphasis on safety to exceed 1 million man-hours without lost-time accident.
10. Maintain housekeeping at the level of	100%	99%	99.5%	99.25%	Continue present emphasis.
11. Attain a cost reduction goal of	$55,301	$12,508 (26% attained)	$62,490 (113% attained)	$74,998 (139% attained)	Through May, revised goal: $145,691.

GENERAL FOODS CORPORATION

Position Description

POSITION TITLE: Director, Area Operations.

UNIT AND LOCATION: International Division (basic). REPORTS TO: President and General Manager.

Purpose. To plan and direct execution of overall business of the area subsidiaries, in keeping with divisional objectives.

Major responsibilities and end results expected. Subject to the general guidance of established corporate and divisional policies, the incumbent will:

Direct the overall operations of General Foods in assigned areas to insure all reasonable steps are taken to conduct these operations in an efficient and profitable manner, delegating responsibility to managers of subsidiary operations.

Formulate, recommend, and participate in determination of policies and goals to insure they are in accordance with the unique characteristics of the area: competition, existing facilities, problems arising from governmental contacts, ways of doing business, laws, taxes, habits of the people, and local economic conditions and trends. (Also to represent the corporation in major acquisition negotiations.)

Evaluate, recommend, and/or establish long-range plans and annual and interim profit plans for the purpose of forecasting the anticipated potential of the area operations in terms of expected profits and preparing set objectives to this end.

Review and evaluate performance to insure maintenance of optimum performance in terms of expected potential and to identify problems and recommend necessary corrective measures.

Select staff personnel and plan development for the purpose of maintaining the area manpower requirements at a sufficient level of proficiency to meet objectives.

NOTES TO CHAPTER 4

1. "Management by Objectives," General Policy and Procedure, New Holland Machine Company, Division of Sperry Rand Corporation, March 15, 1965, p. 1.
2. McConkey, Dale D., "Judging Managerial Performance: Single Vs. Multiple Levels of Accountability," *Business Horizons*, Fall 1964, p. 50.
3. *Ibid.*, pp. 50-51.
4. Schleh, Edward C., *Management by Results*, McGraw-Hill Book Co., Inc., New York, 1961, p. 22.
5. Juran, Joseph M., *Managerial Breakthrough*, McGraw-Hill Book Co., Inc., New York, 1964, p. 44.
6. Schleh, Edward C., "The Fallacy in Measuring Management," *Dun's Review and Modern Industry*, November 1963, p. 50.
7. Ewing, David W., *The Managerial Mind*, The Free Press of Glencoe, Collier-Macmillan Ltd., London, 1964, p. 69.
8. *Ibid.*, p. 73.
9. Wertheim, S. E., "Standards of Performance," memorandum, The Cleveland Electric Illuminating Company, November 13, 1963.

5. Supporting Elements

As an integral part of the whole management process, objectives and standards of performance cannot be viewed separately from certain other activities which are of major importance to management. Moreover, the successful use of objectives and standards depends on the smooth functioning of these related activities. This chapter will discuss some of them, beginning with a consideration of budgets.

BUDGETS

A budget is an effort to measure. Budgets are also devices for extending plans in detail and communicating the standards that must be met if the plans are to be realized.

Budgets are thus an important ally of management by objectives and standards of performance. Usually, a company first sets objectives and standards; then it tests their reality by extending them in budgets. If the evidence indicates that the objectives and standards as set are not realistic and feasible, they will be revised. Here occurs a "closed" feedback cycle, in this case the cycling of plans through "model testing" and replanning. This occurs before performance. As

the results of performance appear, a similar recycling takes place.

The importance of budgets to all company· planning is stressed by Dale D. McConkey, vice president and assistant to the president, United Fruit Company.

Financial budgets take into account the things we are talking about, from the top of the pyramid on down, our basic mission and our objectives. And then we consider what each division is going to be doing. What the divisions plan to do influences the group executives, the president, and the chairman of the board. What are they going to do in each particular area this year? What are our objectives?

Then, after the corporate objectives are determined, the general managers go right on through the whole organization: "Well, boys, this is the guideline. Let's go! What do we have to do, each of us, to attain this particular guideline?"

Charles Granger, partner, William E. Hill & Company, added details to his description of one company's typical approach to budgeting.

What we have is a list of the things we would like to do. These constitute our objectives. But we also have certain priorities. So, when we sit down to work on pre-planning our budget, we stretch as many "bucks" as we anticipate we can get. In other words, we make our list with

93

15 objectives rather than ten. But then these go into the budget hopper and things begin getting cut. So we end up recognizing that we are going to have fewer dollars to show in terms of people, or facilities, or what-have-you. This means we must reduce the objectives for the budget period.

That the objectives of the business are the beginning of the planning process and the budget is a consequence is also emphasized by Robert O. Barber, president of Univis.

Our budgets are not an objective, but are the results of objectives. Each year we operate with a minimum budget level (MBL) which represents the amount of money we believe it is going to cost to do a job which satisfies our minimum objectives and in which we have a high confidence level. We also operate with a quota level, which is substantially increased performance. Financial plans are made for both levels of operation and are determined to be possible and practical. Budgets indicate what we expect to spend to get the job done. Within the budget we indicate the most important factors. And these are the standards which represent the percentage of the sales dollar we are willing to spend to get various parts of the job performed. Obviously, the standards are more important to the budgeted amounts, since we are willing to spend more money than we have budgeted if we can get the increased business on standard costs.

J. F. Meagher, management education adviser for Socony Mobil Oil Company, indicates in a brief statement that a similar attitude prevails in his company: "Generally, our budgets are a financial expression of the objectives of the company or a particular unit. They represent the dollar resources to be committed to the attainment of certain objectives. Accomplishing objectives within the budgeted limits is one of the goals our managers are to meet."

American-Standard has included instructions in its policy-and-procedure statement on the matter. Point 2 in the statement brings out the relation of budgets to key result targets:

Key result targeting must be done concurrently with division long- and short-range planning, and the final targets must be directly tied into the authorized annual profit plan of the division.

The basic steps in preparation of key result targets are:

1. Prior to the preparation of the annual profit plan, each manager determines with his supervisor the key results which he must achieve in the budget year in order to make necessary progress toward division and component five-year goals.
2. The annual profit plan is then prepared. The annual profit plan consolidates and documents the result targets in terms of dollars and necessary supporting programs, and may bring out inconsistencies between targets in various departments.
3. After corporate review and acceptance of the annual profit plan, and after appraisal of the individual's performance for the prior year, the tentative result targets are adjusted to conform with the local division plan (budget) as authorized.

THE MANAGEMENT INFORMATION SYSTEM

"Information," in the context of this report, means the result of measurement, including both precise measurements (which vary by minute amounts) and coarse measurements (which may state no more than inequalities). Objectives and standards of performance will effectively guide individual managers only if the results of their efforts are revealed to the managers in timely information for their use in evaluation.

Some reflections by experienced managers on the relationship between objectives (and standards) and a company's information system are relevant here. Otto Greven, vice president of production, Donaldson Company, spoke of these matters from the viewpoint of his company's use of information and control systems. It will be noted that information needed in measuring achievements is designated by the objective-setters but collected, analyzed, and communicated elsewhere in the organization—usually, in the finance department.

Management information and control systems are used in measuring the accomplishment of the goal. We have found that, actually, we are not required to set up a lot of extra records in order to measure our achievements. Normally, the information is available somewhere in the company. At the time we set goals, we also designate information which will be gathered to be used in measuring accomplishment and who is to collect the information. In general, it is most desirable to have our finance department collect the data.

Many of those who were contacted for this research referred to the importance of management information systems to control. One such was G. T. Canatsey, director of management development, Pet Milk Company: "Management information and reporting systems provide the necessary feedback to control operations in line with established targets."

Robert O. Barber, president of Univis, emphasizes accessibility of information and its importance in review:

Each manager within the framework of our company operates with a set of controls which give him instant access to all phases of the operation for which he is responsible. He can find out how many of a certain type of product we produced yesterday, or how many we sold— what the cost of those products was, and the revenues and the profits resulting. Timetables and target dates are established and reviews performed to determine progress being made. The periodicity of the review depends upon the situation. Bottlenecks that develop, if they can't be broken by the responsible individual, are taken to the next echelon of authority for assistance. Quarterly review of standards of performance is standard procedure. Summaries

of findings on these performance reviews are immediately drawn up and go to the next echelon of authority, and at certain management levels these summaries are reviewed by the executive committee.

J. F. Meagher, management education adviser, referred to his (Socony Mobil Oil) company's purposes in using control systems:

Our control systems are designed to provide managers with information concerning their progress (or lack of progress) as they proceed toward goal accomplishment. We seek to establish accountability on the basis of elements within the control of the individual charged with goal accomplishment. Our control systems seek to provide them with the information appropriate to corrective action as the situation demands.

J. T. Gresh (American Brake Shoe Company) speaks of an information system in process of development: "We don't have a computer or sophisticated EDP system. We have been improving our data-handling procedures, though. And we produce the information a man needs to know if he is meeting his standard or not. If a new standard is created and we are not producing the needed information at that time, then we'll alter our information system so we do produce it."

As a last illustration of a company approach, R. M. Davis, personnel manager of Reynolds Metals Company's plastic films plant in Grottoes, Virginia, tells of the information system in use there. It works through procedures detailed in an annual objectives book and three follow-up and control documents which Davis describes as follows:

Plant and departmental objectives (black book). Issued annually with intermediate revisions as necessary. Lists plant and department heads' objectives for the year, together with performance standards for measuring progress in attaining them. Also defines degree of authority granted each level. Purpose: to minimize need for day-to-day, week-to-week direction by helping each man to operate within the framework of objectives selected and authority provided.

Objective performance (red book). Issued monthly on seventh working day. Provides information on profits, return on investment, cost reduction, methods improvement, conversion efficiencies, quality, and inventories, together with various current cost data, including unit costs by plant function. Purpose: to show department heads their current standings in relation to the specific objectives (in black book) set by each of them at the beginning of the year.

Monthly financial report (blue book). Issued on the eighth working day. Gives individual reports and schedules, including condensed balance sheets and operating statements; P&L by major product lines; details of expenses; numbers of employees and payroll amounts; summaries of inventories; and a work sheet showing reconcilement of inventory, cost of sales, and variance relationships. Purpose: to inform plant, division, and corporate management of the plant's financial condition. Same schedules are used by the controller's staff for consolidation and control purposes.

Cost control report (gray book). Issued monthly on tenth working day. Gives detailed comparisons, by types of expense and cost center, of actual monthly costs against budgeted allowances. Contains expense ledger detail, plus excess scrap and material usage data, giving a total conversion cost. The variable budgeted allowances are individually computed each month and added to the current fixed amounts for a sound monthly spending allowance. Purpose: to use responsibility accounting technique by giving detailed cost performance data to individual managers responsible for many of the plant cost elements.(1)

All the preceding quoted statements add up to a general recognition that a management information system should bring out the facts on every objective and standard, without exception. And, as has been said, control

measurements must surround the work plan, to insure effective control.

ORGANIZATION PLANS AND JOB DESCRIPTIONS

Job descriptions, in most cases, are the beginning of a standards of performance program. Since the description is also the job's "charter," it is the basis on which objectives and subobjectives are assigned. There is general agreement that job descriptions serve a useful purpose; although their continued use is to be expected, their character and form will undoubtedly be changed. The permanent part of the description is likely to become shorter, while the part which will present the job's objectives and standards of performance will grow longer.

Opinion on the value of job descriptions is not unanimous, however. Some repondents in this research expressed a viewpoint similar to that of Dale D. McConkey (United Fruit Company):

. . . the more we move to the management-by-results approach, the less we need formal position descriptions or job descriptions. I think we may be moving toward a situation in which we will use these only to spell out the broad areas for which people are responsible. A position description tells you what door to go into if you want to talk purchasing, or industrial engineering, or industrial relations, or whatever it may be.

Many of the position descriptions I have seen, and I am certain you have seen them too, are quite lengthy. They use a lot of general expressions. About the only thing that the majority of them tell me is that if I have a problem in this particular area, this is the man that handles that particular type of problem. I should go to see him. But beyond that I don't believe the descriptions spell out what we are really looking for.

McConkey holds that useful descriptions

should include the specific objectives the man and his boss have set for the period. For him, and for others, these are the important aspects of the job which must be communicated to the members of the organization.

Charles J. Wielgus, director of organization development for Reuben H. Donnelley Corporation, expressed a similar view: "We think job descriptions are going to be sharpened up, and may be improved to include such things as freedom to act in addition to what results are expected. And we think they will become more of a multipurpose instrument. In our company, we think that this will come about because our particular form of compensation program puts more of a focus on the job description than has existed in the past with us."

Wielgus also stated his expectation that the description would have to be sufficiently detailed to have the information necessary for organization clarification, job evaluation, recruiting and selection, job orientation, and training.

R. O. Barber, president of Univis, described his company's approach to the use of job descriptions in the context of implementing long-term plans and providing guidance for the assignment of objectives:

All employees of the company work with job descriptions. These job descriptions are the fragmentations of the job to be done, and we attempt to delegate the proper authority to discharge the proper responsibility in each case. Our organization plan exists for each year, and we are now revising our plan to have it more fully reflect organization requirements throughout the life of the five-year plan. Obviously, the organization plan and job descriptions [represent what is needed for] adequate performance of objectives.

Gerry E. Morse, vice president of Honeywell, is still more explicit in describing job descriptions as the foundation on which objectives are based:

Our organization plan and the individual executive's job description are foundations upon which the specific objectives are built. The counsel and guidance of his superior are the devices we use to make certain that a man's objectives do adequately reflect his organizational responsibility and the assignments, both explicit and implicit, of his job.

And another example of the application of job descriptions is provided by G. T. Canatsey, director of management development, Pet Milk Company:

You might be interested in knowing that we have been using the RIG (responsibilities-indicators-goals) approach to establishing individual goals. We take the job description, develop indicators of performance (ways the performance of each responsibility can be measured), and from these develop goals or targets (possible accomplishments needed to meet department or division objectives). This method anchors goals to individual responsibilities—and when these are tempered by the unit's objectives, there is a common relationship between the individual's goals and those of the organization.

The form reproduced on page 92 is part of a job description developed and used by General Foods Corporation. Such a one-page statement, if supplemented by lists of objectives and standards of performance, represents what the cooperators in this research described as "a trend."

PERFORMANCE APPRAISAL
AND MANPOWER DEVELOPMENT

The weight of evidence indicates that appraisals are being based more often on objectives, or on performance standards which, as noted previously, are usually derived from job descriptions. Within the limits set by human frailty, a consideration of personal traits, or knowledge, or skills, does not enter into the appraisal situation.

A recent National Industrial Conference

Board survey of 52 companies found about two out of five firms using what they call "the job-oriented method," which appraises by means of lists of job responsibilities against descriptions of what has actually been done to fulfill the responsibilities.

Other companies are using a technique they call "goal setting," which adds to the job-oriented method specific, scheduled objectives which have been agreed to by the manager and his supervisor. The NICB report thus summarizes current attitudes on goal setting:

Those endorsing goal setting readily concede that there are difficulties: specific objectives, especially for some management positions, are extremely difficult to define. And then there is resistance. But all in all, they say, the results of goal setting are worth many times the effort.(2)

And Dr. Earl R. Zack, professor of management, Graduate School, Pace College, reporting the results of a study of the performance appraisal programs of 50 major companies which was conducted for the Executive Research Conference (an activity of the Pace College Foundation), wrote: "The organizations surveyed almost uniformly stated their conviction that company goals or objectives should be the basis of managerial performance appraisals."(3)

A number of the respondents who cooperated in the AMA research supplied statements of the purpose of their appraisal programs, or descriptions of the techniques employed in carrying out the programs.

Transcon Lines

Allan B. Foy, vice president of industrial relations, described the aims of Transcon's appraisal program in these words:

A semiannual appraisal is conducted in June and December of each year for all salaried employees. The objectives of this program are to:

1. Establish concrete goals and objectives on an annual basis for all salaried employees.
2. Develop salaried personnel to prepare them for increased responsibilities within the organization.
3. Institute a management inventory and audit to enable the company better to evaluate the capabilities and potential of individual salaried employees.
4. Create a rapport and greatly improve communication between supervisor and subordinate.
5. Establish firmly the concept of salary increases granted only as a reward for outstanding results obtained through improved job performance.

Socony Mobil Oil Company, Inc.

J. F. Meagher, management education adviser, said of the Socony Mobil program:

Sound performance appraisals are the basis for manpower development and effective salary administration. We desire to have our people appraised on the basis of the results they have achieved versus those expected of them, taking into consideration the conditions which had an impact on their work performance. We seek to minimize subjective influences such as personal traits or characteristics.

The Boeing Company, Aerospace Group

Max Canterbury, senior coordinator, management development, reported Boeing's conviction that objectives are the useful technique in both appraisal and development. His statement says a great deal in a few words.

Since objectives state specific results to be accomplished, they are more useful in appraisal and development than are job descriptions, which indicate generalized results. Objectives are a good basis for developing a person because the man and his superior, having reached prior agreement on where the manager is trying to go, can more readily agree on the skills and abilities he should strengthen to get there.

American-Standard

American-Standard provided a more detailed discusssion of its performance appraisal program, which is a practical model of what most respondents consider the most useful and effective approach. The program has been used for about seven years, but it still has one problem that plagues appraisal generally. On this point E. M. Campbell, manager of manpower development, commented:

The most difficult problem in installing this program and continuing its effectiveness is overcoming the interpersonal blockages that are inherent in any results-oriented appraisal system. From a positive point of view, we feel the program does bring to life a limited amount of performance appraisal on an annual basis. It tends to produce a greater understanding, among members, of their people's responsibilities. However, we believe this is quite slight, and not effective from an overall corporate point of view.

So we see that, although results are better than those obtained with techniques used in earlier years, current practice has not quite solved the performance appraisal problem. Other knowledge and skills are required. Campbell described American-Standard's efforts to acquire them:

Our plans for further development of these management procedures center around what we choose to term "organization development," an attempt at total organization improvement in the management of people. Using behavioral science research and techniques, we are attempting to reduce interpersonal blockages and improve listening and candid, open communication.

Despite the problems, there is strength as well as thoroughness in American-Standard's approach. Excerpts from the company's policy statement, "Appraising the Performance of Exempt Salaried Employees," are reprinted here at some length because of the exceptional clarity and attention to planning that they reveal.

1. To locate opportunities for improvement in present performance of individual jobs.
2. To locate individual training and development needs and assist in determining action to be taken.
3. To assist in determining qualifications for transfer and promotion.
4. To establish eligibility for increased compensation (merit increases and extra compensation), if applicable.

The method described herein consists essentially of the following steps for each job each year:
1. Establishing specific key result targets.
2. Recording actual results attained against each target.
3. Determining those areas of performance which are good and those which need strengthening, by analyzing why actual results varied from target.
4. Developing an action program of work experience and training through which the individual can strengthen his ability in those particular areas.

A manager must, of course, be appraised on his total responsibility. At the same time proper emphasis must be given in each period to those particular problems and improvement needs in his area which must be met if the enterprise of which he is a part is to prosper and grow.

Thus, a manager's result targets must both pinpoint current problems and needs and at the same time be collectively broad enough to cover his responsibility.

Carrying out the steps listed above with each of his subordinates is, of course, an inherent part of any manager's job and would have to be done in some manner whether this particular procedure existed or not.

The intent of this policy is to provide the

simplest possible means of formalizing these steps so that there will be an adequate factual base for manager development, promotion, and compensation.

The responsibility for measuring progress is set and the frequency of reviews is scheduled:

Accurate records of accomplishments against targets shall be maintained. In most cases, such records should be available in control reports. Where these reports do not provide required information, it shall be the responsibility of the manager concerned to maintain such simple records as will accurately reflect his accomplishment.

In the normal course of business the individual and his supervisor will discuss progress in achieving targeted results quite frequently. In any event, a discussion should be held at least quarterly on each target operative during the period. In these discussions, the supervisor and the individual should consider any problems that stand in the way of full accomplishment of targets and decide on necessary action. These discussions also provide the supervisor with an opportunity to comment on good performance.

The year-end performance appraisal is the formal, overall review:

1. *Preparation.* At year-end, in order to pull together and document the appraisal data and development plan and insure that accomplishment on all assigned targets has been reviewed, the supervisor will schedule a performance appraisal interview with each of his subordinates. This should be a confidential discussion between the individual and his supervisor, the substance of which will not be communicated except as provided herein.

One week before this interview, the subordinate will submit to his supervisor, on the form provided for the purpose, a statement of his previously authorized targets and his actual accomplishments against each of them, together with appropriate comment. [The form also includes space for comments by the executive who makes the appraisal.]

This form, comparing results expected with results actually achieved, provides the framework for the interview.

2. *The Interview Itself.* The primary purpose of the appraisal interview is to help the subordinate better understand his performance strengths and the particular skills, knowledge, and experience which he should acquire in order to improve his performance in the areas where he is not so strong.

The end result of the interview should be a development action program which the subordinate and his superior will carry out in order to strengthen his performance.

Most subordinates are reluctant to admit any needs for performance improvement unless they are confident that the supervisor will use this knowledge in a constructive way. Therefore, the interview should be of the problem-solving type in which the supervisor makes clear that he is looking for ways to help the subordinate achieve even better results, rather than looking for opportunities to criticize and reprimand.

Also, the supervisor should so plan his meeting with each subordinate that there will be sufficient, uninterrupted time to accomplish the purposes of the meeting—normally, two to four hours.

The subordinate should be encouraged to do the majority of the talking and presentation of information on accomplishments against targets. The primary function of the supervisor in the appraisal interview is to be a questioner who is interested in why performance exceeded or fell short of expectation.

The following are the kinds of questions a supervisor might use in an appraisal interview:

  a. What is your evaluation of the results you achieved? If any targets were not met, why?
  b. In the light of subsequent events, were these the right targets? Were they too easy or too demanding? Should different targets have been selected? What obstacles were there in achieving them? What unforeseen situations affected your accomplishments?
  c. What do you think you did particularly well—not so well—why?

d. What action can you, I, or both of us together take to capitalize on the things you have done well, and to improve your performance in other areas?

At the close of the interview, the supervisor should summarize the appraisal orally, indicating:

a. Strengths as revealed by the appraisal, with appropriate commendation.
b. Particular areas of knowledge, skill, and experience which need strengthening. (No employee should be told his particular ranking in the "overall" evaluation; that is, below standard, standard, above standard.)
c. Agreed upon, tentative action steps to secure improvement in each area.

3. *Written Statement to the Man.* The supervisor should, normally, write a summary to the subordinate, in which he confirms the previous oral statement of performance strengths and areas needing strengthening. He should also detail the development action plan which will be followed.

American-Standard closely integrates profit planning and performance appraisal; therefore the first tentative statement of result targets is completed before the preparation of the annual profit plan. And the final, authorized result targets are agreed to immediately following authorization of the annual profit plan and completion of the performance appraisals for the previous year. This is done no later than January 15 near the beginning of the company's planning year. This quality of integration is one of the major values of American-Standard's appraisal program.

International Telephone & Telegraph Corporation

ITT also has a unique approach to performance appraisal. The program the executive personnel department is installing in the company's worldwide operations also entails a close integration between business planning and performance appraisal. Their program, as Dr. Ronald Casey, administrator, executive development, describes it, represents the present trend in performance evaluation. Casey's description of their program is therefore of fundamental interest.

Our department, executive personnel, has the staff responsibility for about 1,300 executives in ITT's worldwide operations. Most of these men report to a division general manager or above.

Our performance appraisal program is based on a management by objectives approach. It has been used worldwide since Fall 1964. Prior to that, it had been applied in a few of our North American divisions; the experience with these programs led to its application on a worldwide basis. Mr. Geneen, ITT's chairman and president, introduced the program throughout the ITT system by a statement of policy addressed to all division chief executives. He emphasized that the evaluation of executive performance is one of the most important responsibilities assigned to top management. As a follow-up to Mr. Geneen's letter, executive personnel members visited all division heads to help in the installation of the program. In advance of the personal visits, division chief executives were asked to prepare preliminary appraisals on all the men reporting to them in 1964. We sent along samples of completed evaluations [page 103 of this report] so they could see what was called for. The samples served as guidelines. Since the program was introduced in the latter part of the year, this meant, of course, that they had to create after-the-fact statements of the significant goals which had been worked on during the year. Although some found this to be a difficult task, it helped to pave the way for the advance setting of goals and objectives for 1965.

As you would expect, when we initially visited field units, we found great variability in what had been done on a preliminary basis: Some of the general managers had very complete statements and objectives, while others had the very sketchiest of outlines.

Before we visit a division to work with them

on their performance evaluation program, we study the detailed business plan for the unit. Since the appraisal program encourages the general manager and his staff to work from their business plan to develop objectives and major individual assignments, we want to familiarize ourselves with the unit's overall goals. We have access to the business plans for all units; usually, a member of the executive personnel group participates in the review of the plan when the general manager presents it for corporate approval.

As part of our visit to a division, we emphasize that the program is designed to be of value at the local level: essentially a work-planning device to help executives to identify the major actions which are needed to attain the unit's overall sales and profit objectives. Approaching it this way, we anticipate a comment made frequently: "I'm not interested in an historical record of past performance. I know what we did then. If I complete an evaluation for you, it is only to let you know how each man did, and this isn't very helpful to me. What I'm interested in is what they will do next year."

One of the things we have found is that some managers prepare too many goal statements. We ask them to concentrate on the few goals that are really critical to achieving the unit's business plan. In this way they are encouraged to do a good job on a limited number of critical items rather than diffuse their effort among many goals of widely varying importance. This, of course, is a matter of judgment. And, by the way, we have no system for weighting goals to show relative importance or priority; nor do we use, as such, shared or joint responsibility for goal accomplishment.

When the program was first introduced, we worked with the managers and helped them in their initial attempts to state objectives and expected results. We assisted them in adopting yardsticks on measures which they could use to judge how well a particular task was performed.

Sometimes a general manager will ask why he should send completed year-end appraisals to New York (ITT headquarters), particularly since the program is supposed to be primarily for his benefit. We explain that, while the program is designed to serve at the local level,

we also get value in New York. Succession planning is one thing we mention; promotions and transfers are others. And, importantly, the appraisals are used to help top management in their consideration of base salary and incentive compensation decisions.

Managers differ, of course, in their willingness to use the entire rating range. We're continuing to work toward improving the distribution of ratings in certain units. As a result of the way the program is structured, however, we don't think the difference among managers, in either toughness of goals or leniency in appraisals, makes a great deal of difference. In making cross-unit comparisons, we judge the appraisers and also compare the appraisal judgments with the actual, overall business results achieved. This helps to put things in perspective.

There is one objection we sometimes hear, and that is the time our approach requires. We answer this by emphasizing that what they are really being asked to do is sketch out a systematic plan for utilizing their management resources. Since developing statements of objectives takes a great deal of time, most general managers are quick to realize that this process can begin by having the subordinate first prepare them. Then the man gets together with his boss so they can reach agreement. The operating people like this approach.

One of our divisions has developed a useful system. It prepares a booklet which shows for each management position the position title, responsibilities, and specific statements of objectives for the current year. These are developed from their business plan which highlights the major unit goals and the strategies for their accomplishment. The book is seen by all the managers. It is a reminder of what each must do if the company is to accomplish its business plan. But also it tells each manager what the others are doing; it's an effective communications tool.

And one last point. I know I have already said this, but I repeat it for emphasis. The objectives we set are for a calendar (also fiscal) year and are for critical events. We ask our people not to attempt to cover all of a man's job responsibilities. We assume that the routine aspects of a man's job will be handled acceptably. If he falls down, he'll become aware of it. Or it will become an objective.

INTERNATIONAL TELEPHONE & TELEGRAPH CORPORATION

Performance Evaluation (Senior Accountant)

SPECIFIC PERFORMANCE ANALYSIS

Major Assignments and Expected Results: Describe the individual's major assignments, specifying agreed-upon goals, work schedules, quality standards, etc. Describe the expected outcome of the assignment in terms of performance standards and objectives by which you judge adequacy of execution. Where possible be objective; that is, profit after tax, report-completion date, cost reduction, ($) goal, and so forth.

Results Achieved: Describe the actual outcome of the assignment in the same terms as in column 1. Where possible indicate factual data supporting your judgment of achieved results. Indicate also factors beyond control of the individual which affected performance on each assignment. Consider changes in performance standards, emphasis, timing, duration, etc.

1. Prepare accurate monthly reviews of consolidated net income estimates by deadline date. *Yardstick:* Accurate monthly reviews completed by the tenth of each month.

1. All monthly reviews were completed by deadline date.

2. Prepare data required for annual report to Securities and Exchange Commission. *Yardstick:* All necessary data prepared and submitted with no kickback from S.E.C.

2. All necessary information was prepared. Submission requirements were properly interpreted despite several changes in content of required materials.

3. Develop a checklist which can be used to guide and verify the completion of required documents for inclusion in the annual report. *Yardstick:* Checklist to be available for use by September 30th.

3. Checklist was submitted by August 1. All necessary items were included.

4. Prepare quarterly consolidations for submission to banks and insurance companies. *Yardstick:* To be completed by the 15th of the month following the close of each quarter.

4. In the third quarter consolidated statements were not prepared until the 28th of the month. This delay was somewhat understandable because of a heavy workload of special assignments.

5. Follow up late reports and incomplete budget figures so that consolidated statements can be submitted by deadline dates. *Yardsticks:*
   a. Evidence of follow-up steps taken to obtain required information.
   b. Avoidance of late reports.

5. Adequate follow-up measures were taken and delays in reporting avoided.

OVERALL PERFORMANCE EVALUATION: Indicate your overall evaluation of the individual's performance based on the information developed above. Be sure to summarize those factors in his performance which have played a major role in your evaluation.

EVALUATION OF POTENTIAL: Identify the individual's capacity for advancement on short- and long-range bases. This appraisal may include reference to personal characteristics which have entered into judgment of his potential. In every case give a brief exposition of the steps that are being taken or planned for the further development of the individual.

Detroit Edison Company

S. F. Leahy, Detroit Edison's vice president, personnel, was succinct in characterizing his company's practice:

Our approach to performance appraisal is in terms of goals. We consider all the responsibilities in a job, but naturally we emphasize goals. Most goals are set for a calendar year. These are discussed by each supervisor with the person to whom he reports in what we call the annual planning interview. Goals for each group tie in with overall company and departmental objectives. The formal appraisal is completed every two years to determine the current needs and potential of the individual.

The B.F.Goodrich Company

Arthur K. Brintnall, director, organization development, described the application of management by objectives to performance appraisal as Goodrich does it.

Our performance appraisal program is job-oriented, particularly for our key executives. Each man develops six to ten position objectives for the year. After the position objectives are reviewed by the supervisor and accepted, they become official. During and at the end of the period, results on each objective are compared with the desired results. The overall assessment is a matter of judgment, but the emphasis is on achievement of objectives. This approach is well accepted by our operating people because they feel it is very valuable. The results are tied closely to administrative decisions. This puts teeth in it. Also, it is basic to the administration of the incentive compensation plan.

The Western Company

As noted earlier, The Western Company has developed very comprehensive statements of measurements and standards of performance. A form used in appraising exempt employees is shown below. It is a useful guide to the application of this kind of appraisal technique.

THE WESTERN COMPANY

Standard Practice Instructions: Performance Appraisal (Exempt)

NEED FOR POLICY

The establishment of a policy on performance appraisals and compliance with the policy by managers accomplishes the following:

1. Assures that attention and emphasis is given by the manager to specific responsibilities and concomitant measures for accountability and standards for measuring.
2. Assures appraisal before the adjustment of salaries.
3. Assures that the employee's performance has been discussed and reviewed with him at least once a year.

DEFINITION: There are many types of appraisals and many connotations placed upon each type. One type is an appraisal of the man which relates to self-development planning. Another is an evaluation of the man—whether he stays on the job, advances, is put on a less responsible job, and so forth. This appraisal and evaluation may be done together or separately. For purposes of classification: this policy does *not* relate to these types of appraisals or evaluations; it relates to performance appraisals defined as the appraisal by a manager of the actual results obtained by an incumbent compared with the standards formerly agreed upon for measuring for accountability for each responsibility in the position guide, and for the total job performance. This appraisal of performance relates to what the job *accomplished* is worth in pay. The appraisal is distinct from a performance review discussion with an individual.

FREQUENCY OF APPRAISALS: Managers will conduct performance appraisals to review employees' performance as to results obtained over a specific period of time. No attempt will be made to stipulate the frequency of performance appraisals required for individual cases. The necessity for periodically changing the standards established for measuring accountability makes it necessary that some positions be reviewed more often than others. Also, special attention may be given to a few selected responsibilities during a specific period (for example, quarterly). If results obtained during the period are satisfactory, attention may be given to other specific responsibilities over another period of time.

STATEMENT OF POLICY: It will be the policy of The Western Company that all exempt employees will have a performance appraisal at least once a year.

RATING

The requirements of a managerial or nonmanagerial job as set forth in the position guide provide the only reliable basis for judging performance. Therefore, if the position guide with the measures for accountability for each responsibility and standards for measuring has been clearly and objectively defined and understood by the employee (manager or nonmanager) and his manager, then the employee should be able to appraise his own performance and arrive at the same evaluation as his manager.

Appraisals are inherently subjective. To the greatest extent possible, efforts should be directed toward making them objective. Agreement in advance between a man and the manager to whom he reports on measures for accountability and challenging but realistically attainable standards should make appraisals objective. A good indication of success is when each evaluates results separately but both are in agreement.

Performance in a position can range over a wide spectrum, from the borderlines of acceptable to outstanding. The salary range structure designed to compensate for contribution to the enterprise is such that anywhere in a 35 percent range the work is satisfactory. One problem in salary administration is evaluating performance within that range. The compensation plan is designed so that the minimum of the range is fair compensation for a satisfactory and acceptable performance. The median of the range is the normal compensation for completely filling all requirements of the position. This is the normal level for an experienced person doing all that is required of the position. Some persons will exceed these requirements, as measured by performance. Either they will do the work faster, or with less assistance and guidance, or with better decisions resulting from experience but will be leveling off in this position; or they will be doing more than required work and will have demonstrated capability of assuming responsibility of greater value in another position. Such situations call for compensation above the median and may often call for plans for promotion out of that position.

Evaluations will be graded on a scale from 1 to 10.

Learning; temporary, trial period.	
Satisfactory but minimum acceptable.	1
	2
Needs some help from manager.	3
	4
	5
Performs responsibilities of position guide to approved standards.	6
	7
Above position requirements.	8
	9
Outstanding. Red circle.	10

NOTE: An employee may have been appointed to the position even though he could not carry all the requirements of the position, because he was the best man available and had potential to grow into the full requirements in less time than it would take to train a new man. He still rates less than minimum acceptable. This is no discredit to the man; he must be so rated because in the concept we are striving to adopt we are paying for results of the job, and when such results are not forthcoming we must pay less. In such cases, a temporary position guide should be prepared and an evaluation of the temporary position should be made.

Performance appraisals may be given with or without the employee receiving an adjustment in salary. Normally an employee at the median of his salary level range will not warrant an increase in salary unless his performance is above normal to outstanding.

PROCEDURE

The basis for having a successful performance appraisal is a well written and accurate position guide with its concomitant measures for accountability for each responsibility and standards for the measures which have been mutually agreed upon by the manager and the employee in the position. By using plans, budgets, P&L statements, observations, and reports, the manager and employee can evaluate the employee's performance fairly accurately and objectively. The appraisal should be based on work results obtained through performance of the individual against standards mutually agreed upon and not on personal traits. Comments on an employee's personal traits or habits should be restricted to those cases where such factors are known to contribute to poor or unacceptable performance.

The initial step, of course, is for the manager and employee to have a mutual agreement on the position guide, each having a clear understanding of the responsibilities, measures for accountability, and standards.

The manager will then have a formal performance review with each of his employees at least once a year, or more often when the manager decides more frequent reviews are necessary. The manager should also consider the possibility that the standards for measuring accountability may change from time to time. Any changes should be clearly understood by the employee and the manager at the beginning of the period. A manager will not normally appraise an employee at one time on all of the responsibilities contained in his position guide.

Before the appraisal interview the manager should spend sufficient time to gather facts about results that have been obtained for each responsibility that will be covered in the interview. The interview should be conducted more in a question manner rather than by a statement or direct approach. Skillful handling of questions regarding results obtained versus standards will enable the manager to draw out from the employee the same conclusions as to his own performance as the manager possesses.

The manager should make whatever informal notes that are necessary for his personal use in a follow-up, but formal notes or recording of data discussed in the interview should not be typed and sent to other managers or to the personnel office or maintained in any company files.

The manager should keep the following purposes and precepts in mind while preparing for and during a performance appraisal interview.

1. There should be a complete meeting of minds as to the employee's performance in his present job.
2. Many individuals may be performing extremely well to outstanding in their present positions but are not promotable, either because the individual does not desire to be promoted or because he may not have the qualifications for the next position.

3. The standards established for the individual position may need changing. The performance appraisal interview affords an opportune time for the manager and individual to discuss and agree upon revised standards.

4. In measuring performance against results the manager applies judgment as to whether results are of such a nature that they will be likely to continue; then the manager has an opportune time to discuss salary adjustment. Appropriate performance with an increase in salary may provide for better performance in the future.

5. Since a position guide reflects the responsibilities of a job, managers may have some individuals who are not at present performing according to minimum standards. In such cases there should be a program of self-development planning in which individuals, assisted by their manager, will prepare a self-development plan satisfying their personal objectives. Then the manager should observe the employee's performance very closely to ascertain if the employee is in the right job or not.

Westinghouse Electric Corporation

As shown in detail in Chapter 4, Westinghouse has long had a management by objectives program. A form this company uses in comparing performance against objectives is reprinted on page 108.

SALARY ADMINISTRATION

"What a man makes should be tied to what he contributes to the company. If he produces, he gets; if he doesn't, well—!" This statement summarizes the survey participants' attitude toward salary administration. And it states the fundamental reason why more companies are using achievement of objectives and standards of performance to determine salary action.

The implementation of this attitude toward managerial compensation has increased the use of incentive compensation programs. The size of the pool of money from which the incentive payments are made is determined by the company's profitability. The size of the payment to the individual is determined by his level of responsibility, his base salary, and the extent to which he achieves his objectives and standards. The methods by which this process is effected vary among our respondents,

but there is impressive agreement on its value.

Salary adjustments are being questioned closely. When increases in salary reflect significant improvements in an individual's general performance level, broad capabilities, or potential for future growth with the company, they are judged appropriate; but when they are granted to reward only short-term performance, they are viewed as questionable. Majority opinion among the respondents favors incentive awards as more suitable for short-term aspects of performance.

Discussions between a man and his supervisor concerning compensation are markedly different when they are based on management by objectives and standards; compensation and work planning can be discussed together. But when such a discussion follows the pattern of the traditional counseling session involving a review of the man's personal characteristics, the subject of compensation is usually kept out of it. Our research indicates that fewer companies now show as much concern to separate a review of an individual's performance, based on objectives and standards, from discussion and decision about his compensation. The prevailing attitude is that the individual is paid to contribute to the com-

EXHIBIT 8. *Form Used in Comparing Performance Against Objectives (Westinghouse Electric Corporation)*

Westinghouse

MANAGEMENT DEVELOPMENT

MANAGEMENT PERFORMANCE OBJECTIVES

NAME (LAST)   (FIRST)   (MIDDLE INITIAL)

DEPT. – DIVISION OR ZONE – LOCATION

POSITION TITLE   DATE ASSIGNED TO POSITION

PERIOD COVERED

STEP 1 - List the specific objectives mutually established with the individual at the beginning of the period covered. Include quantiitive objectives and, where appropriate, completion dates.

STEP 2 - Comment on the individual's performance with respect to each objective listed in Step 1.

STEP 3 - STRENGTHENING THE INDIVIDUAL'S PERFORMANCE ON HIS PRESENT POSITION - - Through your observation and discussion of the individual's performance with respect to his objectives, identify and comment on areas where performance is strongest and areas where performance can be strengthened. Then develop specific plans.

A. Comment on areas where performance is strongest.

B. Comment on areas where performance can be strengthened.

C. What specific plans have been made to help the individual strengthen his performance on his present position? List actions to be taken, who is responsible for initiating the action, and, where appropriate, the date by which the action should be started:

ACTIONS   RESPONSIBILITY   DATE

_____   _____   _____
IMMEDIATE SUPERVISOR   TITLE   DATE   NEXT HIGHER SUPERVISOR

pany's performance. When he does, he should be rewarded promptly; and when he doesn't, he should be punished with equal promptness. (The "promptness" of the reward—or punishment—means the period of time following the performance review.) It should be noted that these discussions are job-related, not the traditional performance development counseling sessions.

Donaldson Company, Incorporated

Otto Greven, vice president, production, spoke for his company's policy on salary administration. In rating the individual, manpower development is considered along with goal performance:

In regard to performance appraisal and salary administration, we do not consider goal performance as the sole [standard] of how well a man is performing on his job; for example, manpower development in his department is also important and certainly would be included in the overall rating of the man. However, we do include our goals program in the salary administration of our key people. It appears in our salary program as a bonus plan, and the man included in the program is given an opportunity to earn additional income, depending on the degree of accomplishment of his goals.

The Boeing Company, Aerospace Group

Max Canterbury, senior coordinator, management development, takes a position on job objectives that is somewhat contrary to the consensus. He expressed the opinion that merit compensation and incentive plans should be joined to objectives but that for base salary the job is more important than the objectives.

We feel that the value of the job itself is a more important element in salary administration than is performance to objectives. Some managers set very difficult objectives; others, easy ones. Hence the achievement of objectives

cannot in itself be a criterion for how much the job done is worth. Moreover, most managers are already paid to perform well. Merit and incentive plans, however, should be tied to objectives. These plans must reward outstanding performance of difficult objectives and marked increases over previous objectives. This is a powerful motivator to evoke continuing excellence.

The B.F.Goodrich Company

Clyde O. DeLong, assistant (retired) to the president, enthusiastically endorses the relationship that Goodrich has worked out between position objectives and compensation decisions. The company's position objectives program is designed, in part, as an aid in administering its executive compensation plan:

The position objectives program establishes an objective basis for compensating executives according to their individual contributions to division and corporate results. Although there are several factors that determine the funds available for bonus distribution, an individual's achievement of his annual objectives is of major importance in deciding the amount of his bonus reward.

The position objectives program is also used in deciding on salary action, since the same standards apply: performance against objectives, sustained level of performance, and potential for greater responsibility.

Webb Publishing Company

R. E. Haugan, vice president of Webb Publishing, pointed to the close relationship between achieving objectives and earning a bonus in his company, whose management bonus plan is built on a salary structure which provides a salary range for each position, with intermediate salary steps within the range. An individual's salary level represents, essentially, the long-term worth of his performance. In addition to base salary, this company provides bonus opportunity (a percentage of base salary) for those who are in the bonus plan. The percentage may vary between 20 percent and 30 percent of base salary, depending on the level of the position and the size of the incentive the company wants to make available to the individual. The bonus opportunity is realized by the individual according to his contribution to the company's objectives. Let us suppose, for example, that the bonus opportunity for one job in manufacturing totals $4,175. (See Table 1.) Of

TABLE 1. *Bonus Computation for Three Jobs (Webb Publishing Company)*

A MANUFACTURING JOB

Factors	Bonus (%)	Oppor- tunity($)
1. Production cost (1 year) Minimum 65.5% of labor sales Maximum 62.5% of labor sales	60	2,505
2. Printing division sales volume Minimum $_____ Maximum $_____	20	835
3. Printing division earnings Minimum $_____ Maximum $_____	20	835
Total	100	4,175

A SALES JOB

Factors	Bonus (%)	Oppor- tunity($)
1. Sales volume objective (1 year) Minimum $_____ Maximum $_____	30	900
2. Sales profit objective (1 year) Minimum $_____ Maximum $_____	55	1,650
3. Total commercial dept. sales (1 year) Minimum $_____ Maximum $_____	15	450
Total	100	3,000

AN ACCOUNTING JOB

Factors	Bonus (%)	Oppor- tunity($)
1. Company earnings Minimum $_____ Maximum $_____	25	992
2. Production cost Minimum 65.5% of labor sales Maximum 62.5% of labor sales	40	1,588
3. Accounting dept. expenses Minimum 2.0% of total sales Maximum 1.7% of total sales	15	595
4. Printing division sales volume Minimum $_____ Maximum $_____	20	794
Total	100	3,969

this total, 60 percent ($2,505) will be awarded for effective control of production costs. If production costs run 65.5 percent of labor sales (the sale of man/machine hours), the part of the $2,505 given as a bonus will be a minimum; but if production costs fall to 62.5 percent of labor sales, perhaps all of the $2,505 will be given as a bonus. The same reasoning applies for factors 2 and 3 of the manufacturing job: if only the minimum sales volume and earnings are attained, only a small part of the possible bonus is paid. But as volume and earnings rise, the portion of the possible bonus paid increases. This approach is used for all the jobs covered by the bonus plan. The bonus computations for an accounting job and a sales job are also included in Table 1.

Yarway Corporation

T. B. Palmer, vice president of personnel, recently installed a new management compensation program which is results-oriented in the sense that it relates individual objectives to overall company objectives and gears the payment of individual rewards to success in achieving these objectives. Key features are:

1. All members of management are participants in the program.
2. A single base rate structure has been established for each grade level of responsibility in place of the traditional rate range structure.
3. The concept of merit salary increases has been eliminated.
4. Bonus rewards are dependent upon company profitability and individual performance.
5. The evaluation of individual performance takes into consideration the following factors:
   a. The extent to which overall company objectives have been achieved and the individual's contribution to such achievement.
   b. The attainment of individual performance goals agreed upon by the individual and his immediate supervisor at the beginning of the calendar year.
   c. Accomplishments reported quarterly by the individual to his supervisor.
6. The performance evaluation form used serves as a single common yardstick for evaluating the performance of all participants.
7. The performance evaluation made by the immediate supervisor is subject to review and approval by the appropriate department head and a performance review committee consisting of the president, vice president-personnel, and vice president-finance.
8. The performance evaluation directly determines each participant's percentage share of the bonus fund.
9. The bonus fund is a fixed percentage of the operating profit of the company.
10. The management compensation program is integrally a part of the activities management must perform successfully to achieve company objectives and serves as a means of relating management compensation to managerial performance and results.

NOTES TO CHAPTER 5

1. "Four Books Tell Managers Where They Are, Where They're Going," THE MANAGER'S LETTER, American Management Association, September 20, 1964, pp. 3-4.
2. "Salary Reviews and Performance Appraisals," *The Conference Board Record*, February 1964, p. 47.
3. Zack, Earl R., "Where Are Tomorrow's Managers Today?" *Pace*, Pace College, New York, Fall, 1964, p. 11.
4. "Appraising the Performance of Exempt Salaried Employees," American Radiator & Standard Sanitary Corporation, New York, September 28, 1960.

6. Aspects of the Future

RECENT YEARS HAVE SEEN the advent of much new knowledge which will strongly influence the future of management science. While this does not mean that the future can be predicted, it does mean that anticipating and planning for major developments will be greatly aided in the race to keep abreast of technological change and the ever increasing demands on management. Two additions to management knowledge relevant to this report will be discussed in this chapter:

1. An effective mathematical model of a business as a dynamic system.
2. Faster information-processing systems with higher capacity.

If these new conceptual approaches and information-handling tools are to work effectively, they must be coupled with quantitative objectives and standards. The setting of objectives and performance standards is the critical point of articulation —or, as the military systems analysts would describe it—"the interface," between man and machine.

A BUSINESS AS A DYNAMIC SYSTEM

Any system, as system is defined in Chapter 2, is dynamic if it responds adaptively to either internal or external change.

It is self-evident that a viable business responds to change and strives to respond adaptively.

A business, then, is a dynamic system. But it has been only recently that managers have had the conceptual tools and the information-processing techniques which enable them to manage the business as a dynamic system.

Professor J. W. Forrester of Massachusetts Institute of Technology has been a pioneer in the development of industrial dynamics, the study of a business as a dynamic system. Forrester's developments have resulted from his efforts to fit "the many management functions into a meaningful whole."(1) In his view, the tools of progress are electronic data processing, decision making, simulation, and feedback control. Developments confirm his analysis.

The techniques of industrial dynamics cannot be applied, however, without analyzing the criteria to be made as effective as possible and enumerating the variables and constants to be considered. Key results, objectives, and standards of performance define the criteria, not only for an integrated business but also for each major function of a business and for each managerial job. Since these criteria are identified by managers and applied by managers, the quality of managerial judgment is the critical determinant of the success with which the techniques of industrial dynamics will be applied.

SOURCES OF SYSTEM VARIATIONS

In earlier years, only long experience developed in a manager the knowledge of the sources of system variation—that is, the swings in the rate of change or level of a business's dependent variables which would enable him to make sound operating decisions. Systems research, which leads to the development of a quantifiable model of the business, permits through simulation the study of the impact of changes on the business. Simulation is therefore a partial substitute for experience, but—and perhaps this is of greater importance—simulation also *provides* intensive, guided experience. The result, in either case, is that management decision making becomes more balanced and far-seeing. This reduces the extent of the swings in the measurements of system variables, with a consequent increase in efficiency.

Through the analysis of the variables which are correlated with the criteria—the objectives—we learn which variables have the greatest effect on criteria measures. We also learn how large a change, in rate and amount, indicates valid change rather than random variation. This knowledge, coupled with rapid communication and a response repertoire composed of economic increments, permits the narrowing of the range of variations. The analysis which is required to achieve this end cannot be undertaken without reliable measurements which describe the significant factors at work.

PROGRAMED DECISIONS TO BE INCREASED

When the objectives and standards of the business have been made explicit, and when quantitative models which accurately simu-late the functionings of the business have been constructed, many of the operating decisions of the business can be programed. Many operating decisions will be made by equation, but only because management's decisions on objectives and standards have provided the structure within which the necessary equations could be developed. The objectives are the dependent variables; the activities, the results of which influence the achievement of the objectives, are the independent variables; and the functional relationships among these are the equations. Because of the hierarchical structure of this model, dependent variables at one level become independent variables at another.

Selected values of the dependent variables are preset as choice-points. When the organization's efforts have led to results on these dependent variables at, above, or within the acceptable range, as set in objectives and standards of performance, no change in the pattern of effort is required. But when the results do not meet this test, then there is a choice: Reduce the level of the standard, or change the pattern of resource allocation.

GREATER USE OF STANDARDS OF PERFORMANCE

Quantitative objectives and standards of performance are intrinsic elements of the successful application of business models and high-capacity computers. If, therefore, our prediction that business models and computers will be used to an increased extent in the future is accurate, the need for objectives and standards of performance will also increase. Despite the frustrations inherent in developing sound standards of performance, the work done on standards now is preparation for the effective use of advanced management techniques in the future.

IMPROVED INFORMATION PROCESSING AND DISPLAY SYSTEMS

The fact that information-processing systems of greater capacity and speed will be available in the future is well known; it is a simple extrapolation from the trends of the recent past. But what are the implications of this and other developments in the related technology?

Here are some speculations about the future from J. C. R. Licklider, manager of information sciences, systems, and applications at the Thomas J. Watson Research Center of IBM:

An idea to get used to is that you can sit down at the computer when you sit down at your desk. Your typewriter is connected to the computer and the computer can type back to you when you type to it. The writing surface in front of you is also a display surface, a doodle pad for you and the machine to sketch your ideas on. What used to be in your filing cabinet is now in the computer's store, and the computer displays whatever you designate to it by name or date or label. You can retrieve information not only from your personal file but also, within the limits set by your specified right of access, from the central files of your organization, and you can communicate with your colleagues through the computer system.

The kind of man-computer interaction just described is not here yet in fully operational form. At several universities and in several research laboratories, however, students and scientists are already working daily through typewriters or teletypewriters with digital computer partners. Graphic display and interaction-through-sketching are luxury items now, but in several applications they are proving so useful they have to be afforded. Computer-operated slide projectors and tape recorders and other "interaction devices" are also to be found in some current systems. Thus the computer as a thinking aid exists now, at least in prototype, and we shall soon have a chance to see how it works as an operational tool in various applications.(2)

And an operating executive, Frederick R. Kappel, chairman of the board, American Telephone and Telegraph Company, has suggested what this will mean to the man doing the job:

When we can arrange matters so that everyone in the chain of command can easily know his results by interrogating the machine—when we have constant feedback—then we have a very different situation. Each boss will know from day to day where he stands in relation to where he wants to go, and what is needed to get there. Strengthened by knowledge, he will fret less and lead more. He will be a teacher and communicator. He will be . . . helper rather than overseer.(3)

With sounder judgments as to the objectives of the business, with valid quantitative models of the business, with realistic standards of performance, and with computers and information delivery and display systems of advanced design, the manager will be equipped to manage scientifically. And, since a science yields a more and more accurate picture of reality as its predictions are tested, the manager will manage more efficiently and—hopefully—more effectively.

NOTES TO CHAPTER 6

1. Forrester, J. W., "Industrial Dynamics: A Major Breakthrough for Decision Makers." *Harvard Business Review,* July-August 1958, p. 38.

2. Licklider, J. C. R., "Computers: Thinking Machines or Thinking Aids?" *The New York Times,* May 23, 1965, Section 11, p. 13. The copyright is held by the International Federation for Information Processing.

3. Kappel, Frederick R., executive program lecture, 1965 Management Conference, University of Chicago Graduate School of Business, Chicago, March 17, 1965, p. 3.

Selected Reading

Anthony, Robert N., *Planning and Control Systems: A Framework for Analysis,* Division of Research, Harvard Business School, Cambridge, Massachusetts, 1965. A basic statement of management control theory for operating executives and those engaged in management research.

Beer, Stafford, *Cybernetics and Management,* John Wiley & Sons, Inc., New York, 1959. A highly readable presentation on modern scientific management.

Drucker, Peter F., *The Practice of Management,* Harper & Brothers, New York, 1954. A study of the essence of management in the U.S. business environment today, emphasizing the importance of objectives.

Holden, Paul E., Lounsbury S. Fish, and Hubert L. Smith, *Top Management Organization and Control,* Stanford University Press, Stanford, California, 1941. An early definitive study of top management planning and control practices in 31 major U.S. companies.

Hughes, Charles L., *Goal Setting: Key to Individual and Organizational Effectiveness,* American Management Association, 1965. Working from tested psychological principles, Hughes presents a system for integrating individual and organizational goals. The system is in use in a major U.S. corporation.

Juran, J. M., *Managerial Breakthrough,* McGraw-Hill Book Co., New York, 1964. An excellent statement of control theory oriented to the manager's task.

McGregor, Douglas, *The Human Side of Enterprise,* McGraw-Hill Book Co., New York, 1960. A synthesis of the findings of social scientists which bear on the management of men.

Schleh, Edward C., *Management by Results: The Dynamics of Profitable Management,* McGraw-Hill Book Co., New York, 1961. A "how-to" statement by an experienced practitioner.

Scott, Brian W., *Long-Range Planning in American Industry,* American Management Association, 1965. A scholarly but practical review of current long-range planning practices in U.S. companies.

Index by Company Name